T0368442

GET
WET
AND *Heal*

A Sequel to The Water Kite Journey

DEBBIE TORRELLAS

Balboa Press books may be ordered through booksellers or by contacting:

Balboa Press
A Division of Hay House
1663 Liberty Drive
Bloomington, IN 47403
www.balboapress.com
844-682-1282

Because of the dynamic nature of the Internet, any web addresses or links contained in this book may have changed since publication and may no longer be valid. The views expressed in this work are solely those of the author and do not necessarily reflect the views of the publisher, and the publisher hereby disclaims any responsibility for them.

Any people depicted in stock imagery provided by Getty Images are models, and such images are being used for illustrative purposes only.
Certain stock imagery © Getty Images.

ISBN: 979-8-7652-4174-5 (sc)
ISBN: 979-8-7652-4175-2 (e)

Library of Congress Control Number: 2023908068

Print information available on the last page.

Balboa Press rev. date: 08/09/2023

Get Wet and Heal
A Sequel to The Water Kite Journey

Dedication

As I did with my first book, this sequel is dedicated to my most intimate and precious treasure: **my children**. They opened my eyes to the truth about the real plan in the universe. Their presence in my life pushed me to explore my greatest talents and love. To them, who pulled, pushed, and loosened up my strings through my floating journey, I dedicate every word. My legacy to them is the essence of enjoying life to its fullest and the pleasure of seeing them ride their own journey just being themselves, outgrowing challenges, circumstances, and fears.

I also dedicate my words to those who believed in my dreams and allied with them to make them happen, even when they didn't seem real.

To all my other guardian angels and collaborators in this journey, who have been by my side unconditionally, supporting me with positive energy, floating and flowing with my liquid prosperity.

To every special child who has shared the water with me, teaching me about the other part of life and fun that I had forgotten a while ago, and that I now see available again in daily life.

To the water's inspiration, influence, incitation, motivation, and its wondrous power to awaken my whole being to another level of evolution that connects me to others in infinite ways of love.

To gratitude, innocence, laughter, happy conclusions, and LOVE!

Debbie

Table of Contents

Foreword

My Getting Wet Experience

I have known Debbie, through mutual friends, for nearly twenty years, and have always admired her strong will and determination, as well as her positive perspective on life, regardless of circumstances. These attributes, I believe, are what made her a successful businesswoman and have taken her aquatic therapy practice to new heights.

So, when she approached me to help her with this sequel to *The Water Kite Journey*, I was more than thrilled. I was honored to have been trusted with such a personal project. And I was excited to be part of a natural healing process that was helping so many people, including myself.

Like Debbie, I grew up in Puerto Rico, in sunshiny weather year-round and surrounded by water since my childhood: beaches, boats, cold mountain streams, swimming pools, and even splashing in puddles under the rain (I must confess I've also done this a few times as an adult!!). Therefore, the idea of alternative aquatic therapy sounded very natural to me when I first heard about it, though I had never tried it.

Upon Debbie's urging, I went to her center to get two trial therapies. After all, it was the obvious thing to do if I was going to work on her book. Plus, I was honestly curious to find out how the method worked. I was looking forward to discovering what it would feel like to get therapy while floating peaceably in the water.

As with any novel experience in life, I went into my first session with a bit of apprehension, a bit uptight about how the whole process would evolve. Will it be like a massage? Will they torture me by making me exercise? Will I cause the therapist any trouble?

I must say I was impressed from the moment they put the floaters on my legs, held my head above the water and let my body float freely, with my arms extended, eyes closed, and sunshine beaming on my face. It was a sensory experience I've never had before. It goes beyond the sensation of floating by yourself in the pool or the beach, as we all have done so many times and probably still do. The combination of weightlessness, the subtle ways the therapist moves you around the water and works on different pressure points on your body, all put you into a trance-like state. A thousand random thoughts run through your mind, as if your body and brain were doing a reboot.

I emerged from the initial session in total relaxation, exhilaration and, sincerely, a bit confused as to what had taken place. Why was my body feeling weird, relaxed, uplifted, energized, and tired, all at the same time? How come this was an overall fantastic sensation? I had to come back for more!

After the second trial session, I was convinced I needed to sign up for a whole package of therapies to target several issues I was dealing with physically and emotionally. Additionally, as I said, it would help me immensely in gaining the necessary insights to work on this book.

I soon realized that alternative aquatic therapy is not a fad, nor a new-age invention to try to be different. This is serious therapy, dating back centuries, practiced by professionals in the field, both the field of physical therapy and the more specific one of applying certain techniques that can only work if the body is floating in water. These therapists are licensed and trained chiropractors, specialists in physical therapy, licensed massage therapist and physicians, as well as licensed in Aquatic Therapy. They also provide support throughout the process at the emotional and spiritual level.

I signed up for a formal six-session therapy round, floating twice a week for three weeks. After that, upon looking at the results, we would determine how many more sessions would be needed, if any.

My first formal floating session was, let's a say, a thorough one. My relaxed floating bliss soon turned into a serious pressure point fiesta, expertly applied by two professional lady therapists that made all my muscles release tensions, while all my toxins begged for a way out! It was just what I needed, since one of my goals with this therapy was to begin correcting certain aliments I was experiencing after a major abdominal hernia surgery I had had two years before.

Wow! When the session was over, it took me a few seconds to open my eyes and come to my senses. Remember that weird feeling that I mentioned about being relaxed, uplifted, energized, and tired all at once, and that somehow it all felt fantastic? Well, that happened again, to the tenth power!

As I was leaving the pool, one of the therapists recommended me to take the rest of the day off, go home, have some soup, and relax. Of course, my busy, stubborn mind was rejecting this sound advice, going on and on about all the work I had to finish, how the yard was a mess, how I needed to fix the shower, etc. And, of course, when I got home, the only thing that my body allowed me to do was relax, sit on the recliner watching TV, and have some soup. Lesson learned!

Two days later, I went for my second therapy. This time, it was a gentleman in charge of the session. I thought I would be in trouble, because, being a guy, he would perhaps be rougher on me than the ladies. I couldn't have been more judgmental and wrong! He was another total expert, with an incredible gentle touch. He had even taken the time to find out about my previous session to make sure my body fell into the right rhythm. Soon afterwards, I started to feel more relaxed overall, my chest was beginning to clear out and, over the next couple of days, even my bowel movements began to feel better.

My third and fourth sessions were given by a great lady therapist, who was also a licensed chiropractor. Another expert with a magical touch! I remember the third session particularly, because it was the first time I floated in the rain. The raindrops falling on your face while receiving aquatic therapy is a thrilling sensory experience. The pleasure, and the process of body and mind cleansing, continued.

For sessions five and six, I was back in the hands of the gentleman therapist who I had thought would rough me up. Again, his skills and professionalism shined. He used a combination of pressure point techniques, targeted massage of the back, legs, feet, arms and hands, in addition to moving my extremities gently and fluidly in different directions and positions. It worked like a charm! Not only could I feel my muscles stretch and my joints crack into their right position, but I felt my mind was resting, as if in suspended animation. At the end of these sessions, I felt the same way you feel when you wake up from a good dream; you don't want to open your eyes and face reality, you just want the dream to continue.

I loved the experience and will continue getting wet, as long as I feel I need it. I also learned how important it is to do your part to help the healing process it terms of diet, exercise, and a true desire to get better. No amount or kind of therapy will help you unless you are truly committed to healing.

I understand that each person will need personalized therapies to target their specific needs, and that not everyone may feel what I did floating like a noodle in the water. The main motivation behind sharing my experience is to perhaps encourage others to seek alternative aquatic therapy to treat common ailments, be they physical, mental, emotional, or all the above.

Alternative aquatic therapy was a great discovery for me and I hope more people try it. I look forward to seeing this modality grow and become a science practiced by many for the good of all.

Charles H. Toledo
Writer, Communicator, Translator
and New Convert to Alternative Aquatic Therapy

Introduction

When I considered writing a second edition of my first book, *The Water Kite Journey*, I debated about the direction I wanted to go with it. I thought about doing an entirely new book, with a different spin, new cases, new learning experiences, something to outdo the success of the first edition.

But then it hit me. Why not continue the journey and center it more on the subtitle of the first, *Get Wet and Heal*? After all, alternative aquatic therapy is about healing and transformation, which has always been my mission at **KinFloat Aqua Wellness Center®**.

Therefore, I decided to revamp and reorganize the first edition, add some new cases and concentrate on the healing concepts and advice so eagerly shared in the first book.

You will find in this sequel most of the same information and gracious, fun-loving spirit as before, but sequenced in a way that helps the reader's mind fly smoothly through the process of understanding the benefits of aquatic therapy, its modalities, and the way our own bodies and minds can affect -positively or negatively- our own healing.

You may also find here and there a reference to kites. They are merely a fun throwback to the metaphor of the kite used in the first edition, referring to how one's journey in life could be compared to a kite, flying high or low, sometimes crashing and then flying up again with its glorious colors. But here, I did away with the kite because it also represented a vehicle tethered to a string, a string that holds you back from flying freely, much like an illness holds you back from leading a full life. When we heal, we cut that string, and then we are free to be ourselves again.

So, let's not hold back, let's continue the journey, and let's *Get Wet and Heal!*

Chapter 1

An Invitation to Get Wet

Water is to the body what non-attachment means to the soul,
a clear simple life.

Much has been written about water, and its ancient benefits. So then, what was the value of writing my first book and now this sequel? That was one of the questions I asked myself during my morning walks on the beach.

If I found one answer, it was that I needed to continue writing to go back to basics and share with others the extraordinary wet life experiences that I have witnessed and have faced personally. Another reason was to look at my own experiences of healing people in my island of Puerto Rico, and compare them to the need for healing everywhere. I can confidently say that the aquatic approach to healing is more needed now during pandemic times, where people are emotional and immunologically affected, while feeling confined in isolation, fearing sickness and death.

I also want to raise consciousness about transforming people's nervous system to enhance immunological response by overcoming their mind and the environment in a very simple and practical way, through water. This is an invitation to enhance the power that the nervous system brings to total health. This book is intended to provide faith and hope to heal the body, the mind, and the spirit in the water.

Evidenced-based alternative aquatic modalities used in perfect harmony can help overcome many physical conditions. With this invitation, I want everyone to give themselves an opportunity to gain vitality, self-efficacy, self-efficiency, and self-esteem, transforming any situation considered painful into a magnificent, victorious, and powerful self-bloom. I want to help you take advantage of all the possibilities and resources available to create victory out of chaos. And do this not only with alternative aquatic therapies that ignite transformation, but with the accessory tools we all have inside ourselves that help us sustain a successful healthy life.

Exploring alternative aquatic therapy is for every human soul with a minimum desire to optimize a holistic approach to healing, and for those who love water and have the call to help others.

Embrace personal uniqueness and let the variety of colors, styles, and ways, flow like water does in a magical stream. Explode in good energy, receiving the blessings of the Caribbean sun, or any sun, wherever you might be. Share this journey of acceptance for what it is, and not for what we think it should be. Explore the liquid seduction of water through the change and constant movement of its flow. Enjoy the possibilities present in every moment of life.

Float, allowing the body to show health and wellbeing inside and out, with minimal effort. The purpose is to get wet, to move energy, and eliminate restrictions, allowing the balance and natural equilibrium that aligns the body, mind, and soul to transcend any kind of parameter.

Anything said in this book comes from a very distinct and personal perspective, based on experience, on empirical and scientific evidence, on shared successes and results, and with a special delivery of compassion and love for myself and others.

So, sit back, enjoy and *float*. While doing so, get closer to any water element near you, the sea, a fountain, a river, a pool, a hot tub, or whatever liquid suits you best.

Feel the water move, sit still or just flow, and get really, really wet with the most fascinating element in life, *water*!

Float your worries away. Be ready to feel the love and get wet. Now, have fun and heal!

Chapter 2

Liquid Prosperity

To fly, to float, to dance under the moon,
to swirl through the light embracing life.

By flowing with this book, some will be inspired to discover the most selfish love of all, the love for one's self. Loving the self is accepting the ultimate gift, the challenge or the lesson to evolve in life's journey. Through water, real people transcend to enjoy a richer, successful, and extraordinary existence. Life is fluidity and change. It is unprecedented, unpredictable, never the same. Life is just like water!

The author Mike Dooly speaks wonderfully about the fluidity of life in his book *Infinite Possibilities*. "The manifestation process always works quickly and harmoniously," he says, and this speedy and harmonious movement happens "just as air bubbles from the bottom of the sea always find the fastest way to the surface, unless we get in their way." Simple idea, right? If you disrupt a natural process, it will never flow as it was intended.

Likewise, you should let your natural healing process flow without interruptions. You are as capable of healing as much as you let your personal healing power take charge without being sabotaged by your own thoughts. Just allow your best health to bloom in your mind, let your healthy bubbles find the fastest way to the surface, and enjoy the process.

I want people to feel grateful for everything water can offer, to feel happy for the privilege of just being in this life. And I want them to comprehend the universal place we have in this life from the moment we leave the womb. It is such a great journey!

I enjoy watching people experience every second of their journey, committed to using all the power within themselves, like the talents and gifts the universe intrinsically has given them, sharing them with the community around them. When I do therapy, people think I am doing the healing, but I always make clear that it is their body finding its own balance and connecting them to the best version of themselves.

While floating in water, the body stops whining and starts making changes by simply accepting the abundance within it. Liquid abundance brings positive outcomes, especially when lack of health gives you the most wonderful opportunity to rediscover the big lesson. Floating allows the person to make the decision of creating a better version of themselves.

This is not theory but fact. When you relax, the nervous system can break the wrong neural patterns or connections that have been firing together, sending wrong messages to the body. Suddenly, while freeing the body in floatation, the neural paths find new ways of reminding you of your natural capacity to heal. When this happens, without effort from your body or mind, everything changes for the better, and clarity arises to enhance total bodily function.

The other choice is to just leave everything to chance, but that is just another way of creating a perfect victim. Those who decide to let circumstances rule are the ones who deserve what they have, because their scarcity of thought will not bring anything new, fresh, or good to improve their lives.

All I am sharing here is the vivid experience of my journey through the process of growth, the circumstances and thought patterns that have changed my life and the lives of many people. Discovering prosperity in the water, and discovering love, can lift our essence.

Let me share the experience of a female veteran who served three times in the battlefield. Before starting her therapy, she bluntly expressed how skeptic she was when the doctors at the VA Hospital sent her to my center. Although she is happily married and has a daughter, the PTSD she was suffering made her bitter, extremely distrusting, depressive, and reactive. Plus, she was occasionally tormented with panic attacks.

During her first session, she was protective and very defensive, as if she had closed herself in her own capsule. I therefore decided to apply a very subtle touch, with delicate energy, and slow movements. Little by little, I began to feel her body easing off, almost dissolving like melting butter. I'm being kind of visual here, but it truly felt like that. Then, all her muscles completely relaxed, and her eyes were serenely closed. She was in perfect bliss immersed in the water.

At the end of the therapy, all she could do was cry with happy emotion, while smiling from ear to ear about what she had just felt, and what she heard from the universe during her aquatic therapy. She connected with herself, understanding and feeling compassion for herself and for everything she had lived through. She was surprised to learn that no psychotherapy or medication did for her what the aquatic sessions accomplished. The language of trauma changed to wisdom. She found herself.

From that point on, her life changed and she followed her dream to start something new and beautiful. But more importantly, she learned to honor the loving relationship with herself for the first time in years. The rest of the therapies she received allowed her to create an even more amazing story of success in all aspects of her life. Even her family appreciated her transformation.

And that is why I get wet every day. I do it to enjoy transforming lives through water.

What Does Aquatic Therapy Involve?

Probably, right now you might be asking, What does this lady do in the water? I will try to be brief and clear.

Well, I just play in the water, swaying bodies around as they float, following human tissue and body rhythms, and allowing life to happen. Getting in the water with a client is an occasion to explore and find out what the body needs. It is a moment of perfect of silence, of internal knowledge, the discovery of what that perfect machine wants, without external noises and judgement. Then, the most coordinated dance and exchange of energy occurs between the person being healed and I, opening infinite possibilities of goodness.

Everything happens in short lapses of releases and enjoyment. It reminds me of celebrating life while uncorking the finest and most delicate champagne. You can even hear fireworks in the body celebrating health.

Depending on the thickness and tightness of the weave of the tissue, its sway in the water may be slower or faster, but when the tissue releases, its threads start to feel more delicate and silkier, allowing faster, more graceful movements. As the accurate effectiveness of water can confirm, the body tissue starts moving more freely, capable of achieving magical tricks that can surprise the body. Yet, the person is still not aware of it. When session is over, it is like the end of a fantastically gratifying journey.

That is what I do while practicing my signature alternative aquatic modalities in the water. It is a labor of pure love!

Afterwards, the client transitions to more active maneuvers that require the full action and accountability from the individual to work their body to achieve perfect balance, strength, flexibility, and elasticity. All of this will result in a more passionate and amazing new life. The possibilities are limitless when the will is strong and readily available.

The modality I designed and practice is based on craniosacral therapy, lymphatic drainage, visceral manipulation, energy, touch, and other techniques. These methods are facilitated by the water to help the body find equilibrium with minimal rationalization, and with optimal certainty and trust in one's own body.

There is a difference between **Physical** Aquatic Therapy and **Alternative** Aquatic Therapy. **Physical** Aquatic Therapy is the application of manipulation and exercises that are practiced on land and are transferred to water to make it easier for the therapist to apply. It is also less painful and easier on the client. It is a physical, practical, and clinical solution applied equally to each body part, with the therapist executing patterns commonly used in therapeutic practice. As therapies go, it has a lot of value and complements the healing process.

Alternative aquatic therapy includes the land-based modalities and techniques, but involves the whole body accessing the nervous system, from head to toe. There is solid scientific data supporting the amazing impact that alternative aquatic therapy has over the nervous system. It reboots, organizes and rehabilitates, recognizing the ability of every human being to heal from within.

As Dr. John Upledger mentions in his books and courses, the body is unity. The head holds the treasure of the brain, which happens to direct the synchrony of the rest of the body through the cerebrospinal fluid. It is the master of life and it is the last thing that turns off after death. The whole body is a magnificent machine, and if we give it what it needs to self-regulate in the most profound and simple way, we can achieve extraordinary results.

In the real cases presented in this book, you will discover the most important aspects needed to achieve personal health. The cases will reveal how somatic emotional conditions and circumstances are released during therapy, and how they open new perspectives into recovery and healing. Properly adjusting the nervous system has a great impact on the immune system, elevating its efficiency in releasing toxicity and protecting the body from viruses, bacteria, and other pathogens.

I describe **somatic emotional** conditions as symptoms in the body (**somatic**) resulting from psychological processes (**emotional**). It is simply the way the body accumulates stress in different forms, creating **dis-ease** (meaning lack of **ease**, not so much illness or sickness) in the body. Somatic emotional conditions are the way the body creates uneasiness when the body and the mind are not in sync. This lack of balance will create chaos. By immersing your body in water and contacting your inner physician, you will discover and understand how your body changes when you empower yourself in any situation.

Everything starts from a very personal perspective because health is a very intimate aspect of life. Personal health success depends on many aspects of our own beliefs and values. It takes us just one second to make the right healing choices. But if we don't make those choices, we fail forever, giving circumstances the power to keep bugging us and make our lives miserable. When your health is in turmoil, feelings of powerlessness, tiredness, sorrow, and depression can make your soul collapse.

Finding our mission in life and having the courage to make it happen, regardless of social standards, is a major success. My current mission is being a facilitator of wellness and transformation through water. I would never say I am a healer, but rather a facilitator. I can help or facilitate people to discover what they need to heal by blending fluidity and tissue manipulation in the water. Furthermore, I let the water be an extension of the tissue and allow it to go through its natural healing process.

Those who have had the experience know there is nothing more powerful than water. There is no need, effort, word, or pain that water cannot heal. Alternative aquatic therapy is a perfect safe space of love and compassion, where life starts again, without judgment, just healing. A client once told me, "Doing this one day a month is a lot better than needing a psychiatrist and medication." That is so true! I am not minimizing the value of psychiatric therapy, but healing is a lot more enjoyable within a pleasurable environment and, why not say it, sometimes it is even more effective. That client still comes every week, as he's done for the past six years, enjoying a healthy, prosperous life.

My master of Watsu® and my teacher, Mr. Harold Dull, has always inspired me with a phrase he uses all the time, "Just free the body in the water." And that is the name of his first book, a work of poetry, romance, and love that invites most of the Watsu® family to practice it.

There are other reasons why working in water is so much better. First, from a professional and personal experience, it allows you to freely connect to yourself in a nearly weightless environment. Your sensations and feelings, your healing process, all happen in the isolated ambiance of yourself. This allows you, and only you, to control the outcome. It is an environment of lovely solitude, with multiple sensory deprivations on one side, along multiple stimulations from other senses.

A great advantage of working outdoors in the water, especially in a place as blessed as the Caribbean, is that we enjoy summer-like weather all year long, affording us a safer work environment thanks to the sunshine, the fresh air, the disinfecting properties of chlorine, and the natural physical distancing that can happen in an open pool.

Closed pools, by contrast, can create a toxic environment for the client and the therapist, because chlorine fumes can rise as high as eight feet, which can be harmful if there is lack of ventilation or an ineffective water filtering system. Working outdoors has also been a safe blessing during the Covid-19 pandemic.

From a professional therapist's point of view, when comparing this environment to indoor land therapies, issues such as hygiene in therapy offices must be considered. Land therapists have experienced that therapy rooms are not precisely the most hygienic places to work in. This applies specially to closed air-conditioned areas, which can be contaminated with airborne bacteria, molds, and viruses like influenza or others. Mattresses and other materials are not as clean as they should be. That is one of the most voiced complaints of clients who participate in many therapy offices. And let's consider again how this has been affected further by the Covid-19 pandemic, which has created new hygiene protocols that might not be followed in all cases.

Working outdoors, as opposed to closed spaces, is also more economical; electric bills are lower and there is no need for expensive work clothing or uniforms. And working outdoors allows you to receive free doses of vitamins D and A, which are needed to support your bones with calcium in a natural way. A blessing for both the client and the therapists.

Additionally, warm water reduces stress and pain for the client and for the person who applies the aquatic therapy. As an aquatic therapist, you don't need to deal with people's perspiration and saliva (drooling). You don't need to deal with flatulence, stinky underarms, or feet. Clients take a shower before their aquatic therapy to wash off dirt, sweat, and odors. You are probably laughing at all this right now! But even though people don't talk about it, believe me, it's true!

There are simply too many good and convenient reasons for getting people in the water outdoors!

Water is to the body what non-attachment is to living a clean, simple, and amazing life. A great life is a simple one, flowing in a natural way. Water represents less doing, less effort, less stress, less pain, less work for the body. It is also more awareness of the parts of the body and its mechanics. Water is joy, pleasure, connection, fun, and satisfaction for the body and mind.

I have heard so many times how people started to hear, feel, and understand their body because of their relationship with water. I had client, let's call her Ivonne, who had had two lower back surgeries, and always told me and other clients that I knew her body better than her husband of fifty years! That sounded very flattering, but I would always answer that she simply got to know her body in a more profound way, and that it was her own magnificent body the one achieving all the success.

Water allows the natural transformation of tissue and thought patterns. The body changes with self-knowledge, by awakening self-respect and self-love, and by recognizing useless external attachments that disguise health issues. This process of self-discovery has driven people to understand the authenticity of their health, body, and mind. In fact, success in health can be measured by how effectively we can engage with our body and how we are able to locate the somatic root of pain affecting health, especially when experiencing sorrow and depression. Believe me, it can be done in water faster than we can imagine. Water takes you there, without effort, without talking or trying. Healing just happens and it is so satisfying, you just have to embrace it!

I have another client diagnosed with ADHD, who had thoracic surgery and still comes on a weekly basis, unless he is traveling. He has received several therapies to treat various conditions he had suffered in the past, and has responded extremely positively to our therapy. He has no physical pain now, but he says, "the therapy allows me to be centered and focused on the important things in my life and on my sanity."

The cases shared here are unique stories of clients I have worked with one-on-one, together as a team, to heal in the water. The clients and I share not only a process of "habilitating" the body, but a process of evolution in the journey of life.

Chapter 3

Getting to Know Me

Before we continue with this magical water journey, please allow me to introduce myself. Who am I in a snapshot? I consider myself an extraordinary business woman; an experienced alternative Chief Executive Officer with a demonstrated history of working in the health, wellness, and fitness industry; a skilled holistic health coach and motivational speaker; a successful business owner and instructor; a recognized specialist in the design of retreat facilities and a strong business development professional who graduated from the University of Puerto Rico.

Yes, Puerto Rico.

Puerto Rico is my birthplace, as well as my children's. It is my home, and the place where I have grown personally and professionally. It is an island in the Caribbean that is a territory of the United States. It has a unique population, unlike any in other states or territories of the U.S., or other countries in the Caribbean. In Puerto Rico, we learn and receive our information from the U.S. and abroad. Puerto Rico is blessed with premium waters, magnificent beaches, and perfect year-round weather, which is an added value to maximize health and joy.

Aside from graduating from the University of Puerto Rico, I also had the opportunity to study in the U.S., and have been able to share my work with colleagues from around the world. During these exchanges with other therapists, I realized that my experiences were truly remarkable and quite different from theirs because of the different kinds of health-related conditions that my Puerto Rico clientele brings to me to help them heal. When I go around learning techniques for my therapeutic work, I ask humbly for some advice about specific pathologies. Many of the great teachers I talk to about some of my cases tell me they have never had any experience with those subjects, and they are amazed with the kinds and quantity of pathologies that we see here on the island.

Puerto Rico, because of its nature and culture, is a great human lab, with the best additives to make healing a success. It has a culture of good will, loving kindness, good humor, and strong family values. These cultural traits, unique to our context, can turn upside down any adverse health situation. I am proud to be living and working in a perfect ecosystem for the alternative aquatic therapy profession. We enjoy sunny weather, lots of water, amazingly consistent warm temperatures, a rainbow of skins, colors, and blends, plus a cohesive attitude to help.

In addition, medicine and other health careers in Puerto Rico have been proudly represented abroad in research papers and publications in prestigious scientific journals. We are also well represented in the world by professionals of all types and fields. Given this international exposure, I understand that we are ready to share Puerto Rico's results in water healing with the world. Why not share more data internationally on alternative water therapy? I dare to say that Puerto Rico and water therapy make a glorious combination!

In fact, I can say without hesitation that I am responsible for the creation and formalization of alternative aquatic therapy in Puerto Rico. Developing a full-time aquatic clinic in 2005 was not easy, especially when hardly anyone in the marketplace knew the modality even existed. Slowly, the testimonies from healed clients ignited the curiosity of physicians and other health professionals, who began recognizing the success of our pre-and-post-surgery treatments, and started sending referrals.

Our results are still the best word-of-mouth promotion.

After opening KinFloat® Aqua Wellness Center, we were awarded the Aquatic Therapy University master degree campus certification. We are, in fact, a formal university campus where aquatic therapy students can train and practice, and the only Spanish-speaking campus of its kind in the United States.

Aquatic therapy has bloomed over the past eighteen years in Puerto Rico. We now have more centers and more professionals, including chiropractors and physicians who have been trained by me in aquatic therapy.

It has been a privilege not only creating my own competition, but passing my dream onto a new generation. I am proud of all this expansion. We can say that Puerto Rico is moving forward with the support of science.

Growing as a Therapist

My personal journey with aquatic therapy -receiving, applying different modalities, and customizing water work- has challenged me in many ways.

Everybody and every spirit is different. Therefore, there is no one specific technique to achieve the same results in everyone. The beauty is in the combination of different approaches, always respecting the individual tissue that commands the process.

The therapeutic modalities you will be reading about serve as a guide to understanding my romance and dance with water through a method I have designed to float the body and release its restrictions, the **KinAquaFlow**® method. This method is completely my own adaptation. It merges different modalities without violating the original purpose and objective of each one. This method is designed as a life transformation experience for those willing to go beyond self-healing. It includes a protocol based on craniosacral work (we explain this therapy later in more detail), followed by the application of energy work, plus the use of subtle touch that follows the commands and needs of the nervous system. This is done while facilitating the body's rhythm and tissues with lymphatic drainage and visceral manipulation, myofascial release (if necessary), fluidics, and reflexology, all in one session.

I remember giving therapy to a client from Indonesia who was vacationing in Puerto Rico for three weeks. She came in for just one session to explore our therapies and ended up getting eight sessions in two weeks. She was going through a phase of depression. She's from an original Ayurveda family and was fully aware of self-care. She was amazed with the process and told me, "We do everything you did to me in several separate sessions. In one hour, you gave me five hours-worth of Ayurveda therapies! I am leaving with a renewed life and heart." Two years later, she came back and spend three days a week in my center. She is still a great fan and we continue sharing experiences.

Watsu® (Water Shiatsu) was my "first love" modality because it seduced me into the water and connected me with what I love the most. It changed my practice in many positive aspects.

Watsu® began in 1980, when Mr. Harold Dull started floating people and applying the stretches and principles of the Zen Shiatsu he had studied in Japan, while practicing Tai chi in water. Tai chi is, by definition, a soft movement discipline designed in Japan, which has been scientifically proven to reduce stress, anxiety and improve posture, flexibility and balance. It can also be considered therapy for the therapist if applied correctly.

The interesting aspect of Watsu® is that everything that happens in the receptor during therapy comes from the movements of the feet of the facilitator. How beautiful is that? We can heal another person with the connection and coherence of a rhythmic dance. It still amazes me!

In the Orient, the practice of stretching to open the channels through which our Chi (Qi) energy flows is even older than acupuncture. Stretching strengthens muscles and increases flexibility. Warm water, which is associated with the body's deepest states of waking relaxation, is the ideal medium. The support provided by water takes weight and pressure off the vertebrae and allows the spine to be moved in ways not possible on land. Gentle, gradual twists and pulls relieve the pressure a rigid spine places on nerves, and helps undo any dysfunction this pressure can cause to the organs serviced by those nerves.

The Watsu® receiver experiences greater flexibility and freedom. During Watsu®, a range of emotions can come up and be released in a continuous flow. This reprograms receivers to face life out of the water with greater equanimity and flexibility.

My first encounter with Watsu® was during a session I had paid for at a time when I was saturated and exhausted, jobless, and in physical and emotional pain. In other words, I was burned out. I was not sure what I was getting into. It was simply an impulse to disconnect for a moment and find a change of pace in my life. It was more like a legal escape from everything I was living then.

My therapist at the time was very gentle with me. He placed no timeframe on the session because he noticed my desperation. He patiently followed me in the water for the first 15 minutes of therapy. He understood everything my body needed. He danced with me without imposing anything, at my pace. Then I went underwater, where I spent the rest of the session while he followed my body.

After the session, I cried for three hours. I was releasing three years of pent-up emotions, which were making me sick with pain and depression. I had been wearing my "everything is good" face, playing the "everything is ok, we are doing awesome and we are happy no matter what" persona. I could not stand one more minute of wearing that pretentious social mask. I needed to raise healthy children without sacrificing my pride, my needs, and my ego. I was finally in touch with my emotions and transformed pain into purpose for me and my family. I was saved through water and that was the breakthrough I needed. I needed take off my mask and open my heart to new possibilities. So, I wanted the world to believe that transformation is possible and simple.

Because of this formidable first experience, I used to think that there was nothing more powerful than Watsu®. Then I learned about craniosacral therapy, which I can say made me a better and humbler person, and transformed my practice. Later, I experienced the combination of craniosacral therapy and Watsu® in a session. These two modalities applied at once can sway even the biggest skeptics. The combination feels like magic, and the receiver loses all track of what happened in a very good way, feeling just renewed. Alone and with others, every day I discover a new and more exhilarating romance with water. You can visit **wastu.com** for further information on this modality. There are also excellent resources regarding the effect of Watsu® on PTSD, depression, anxiety, as well as its benefits for athletes and healing warriors.

Craniosacral therapy (spelled *craneosacral* in Spanish), also called **CST** bodywork or therapy, is an **alternative medicine** therapy based on osteopathic principles, designed by doctors of osteopathy in Europe. It explains scientifically how we can connect with our inner physician, who is there to balance and reboot the whole body through the nervous system. The nervous system may have a life of its own, but it integrates all systems in the body.

During a craniosacral therapy session, the therapist places his/her hands on the patient, allowing them to tune into what they call the craniosacral rhythm. The practitioner gently works with the spine and the skull and its cranial sutures, the diaphragm, and the fascia, which is the thin casing of connective tissue that surrounds and holds every organ, blood vessel, bone, nerve fiber, and muscle in place. This way, the restrictions of nerve passages are eased, the movement of cerebrospinal fluid through the spinal cord is optimized, and misaligned bones may be restored to their proper position. This definition is probably an understatement of the possibilities the therapy may allow. If you want more information, surf the web for *craniosacral therapy*. I also recommend the **Uplegder Institute** site, **www.upledger.com,** where you can find a lot of scientific data on its efficiency and healing capacity.

I decided to pursue craniosacral work because of my obsession with trying to understand how my son's brain worked, and how I could befriend and stimulate it to allow him to have a better life, well beyond his special needs. I remember practicing with his head while he was sleeping, because he would not allow me to touch him when he was awake. It was an out-of-this-world experience. It explained to me the perfect energy and rhythm balance of my son, despite his brain injury. He is a grown man now, and is amazing, over and above many people.

I share this story because it helps make sense of this therapy from the scientific and clinical point of view. The craniosacral modality achieves transformation from the inside out through the entire system and all parts of the body.

From craniosacral therapy comes **Bio Aquatic Therapy**, which is done in the ocean with dolphins. Dolphins are amazing creatures that can teach any human the perfect way of a non-invasive approach to the tissue. It is amazing to see how these big creatures have the subtlest and most caring approach to the tissue, achieving impressive reactions.

This therapy activated my assertiveness and my intuition. While I was undergoing my own healing process, dolphins participated in a fantastic way, awakening my respect for nature and their intelligence. Bio Aquatic Therapy combines energy, intuition, and wisdom, shared from the therapist to the participant in a playful way. To know more about Bio Aquatic therapy used by the Upledger Institute, surf the web for *dolphin assisted therapy*.

The Dr. Igor Burdenko Method is my other modality of choice for active therapy. Results are obtained by facilitating and restoring movement by stimulating the nervous system in trauma and sport trauma patients. This method has changed many people's lives, especially when combined with other therapies. You can find more information by searching *Dr. Igor Burdenko Method* on the web.

By combining several of the techniques mentioned above, I created my own method, KinAquaYogi®. We mentioned it briefly before and will talk more about it throughout the book. It has transformed the lives of thousands in a beautiful way. KinAquaYogi® is the combination of all my passions of movement: synchronized swimming, Pilates, swimming, ballet, yoga, breath work, and water polo. Challenging is an understatement; glorious results is what we achieve daily.

Please, do not get distracted by terminology or methods. Just flow and allow yourself to be seduced by water.

Sharing this information on the aquatic therapy field is nothing but my unique journey as a woman who discovered water, healed herself, changed her path in life, and found the mission to coach and cheer for others in similar situations.

I have spent thousands of hours sharing pain and suffering with others, which has allowed me to explore and practice more, to have more to share with others in a profound way. Together, through water, many people have opened their hearts, leaving behind their patterns or false ideas of who they are. These people have discovered their essence, flying over and above every circumstance without fear. Their lives are stimulated with living passion, giving some credit to the big plan of the universe and the divinity within them. I urge people to hear their real self, to observe and rediscover every day as a gift of life. In the end, if they want it, they can all find happiness. And that is what I live for.

Because most aquatic therapy is conducted outdoors, let's reiterate the healing power of the sun and its influence on health. We have been raised to believe the evil side of sun light, so we go around protecting ourselves from the sun, isolating ourselves in air conditioning, and wearing hats and long sleeves.

Instead of that negative image, I want to promote the benefits of the sun, combined with water. The sun feeds the body with light and provides vitamin D, which facilitates the absorption of calcium and other nutrients to keep it healthy. Early and late sun is so good for your health that even gazing at it for a few minutes can fill your body with vitamin A.

Hira Ratan Manek, a sun meditator and guru, states that gazing at the sun every day is "health insurance", even for eye problems. He says that sunlight is an energizer of the brain because it stimulates its maximum usage. We use only 2 percent to 5 percent of our brain, which means we are missing out on most of the given universal mental capacity we possess. The brain needs that sunlit stimulation on daily basis. Here are some health benefits of sun gazing:

1. Activates and regenerates neurons; it's like a natural laser therapy.
2. Activates the "third eye" of intuition, helping us make better decisions.
3. Controls obesity and insulin levels.
4. Stimulates the pineal gland.
5. Improves the immune system.
6. Brings joy and happiness.
7. Improves mood.
8. Improves sleeping habits.
9. Improves eyesight.

Here's a NASA article that provides further information on the benefit of gazing at the sun: https://www.csmonitor.com/Science/2016/1026/NASA-s-decade-of-sungazing-What-have-we-learned-and-why-does-it-matter

Personally, I consider my body a solar energy master. Like all sun worshipers, I wake up with the enlightenment of the sunrise and shut down with the sunset colors. I am as productive as the sun allows me to be. I need the energy of the sun or I am not alive; my energy decreases without it. Sun energy has driven my life. I can spend hours outdoors, sleeping under the sun and never get burned. I feel alive. My body and soul are ignited like a white lightning when I feel the sun on my skin.

While everybody talks about skin cancer and push their fears upon me, I always ask them, What happens with people that work under the sun all day? What about street workers? Birds and ducks? I believe cancer is karmic. We all have the cells, and the sun is not the only thing that ignites skin cancer. I know people that have not been exposed to the sun and developed skin cancer. What about the diets, emotions, and personal behaviors that affect health? I believe that attitude can bring all kinds of fatal sickness to our lives. I understand sickness is within us; we just keep it away with gratefulness, positive thinking, and eliminating rage and fear. While people might see the cancer on my skin, I see instead beauty, warmness, energy, synergy, and health.

Is my skin getting old? The answer is yes, of course! It comes with the territory of living a mission. When the sun touches me every morning, I feel life full of youth and happiness from being warm. I feel I have not aged since my fortieth birthday, when I was reborn to water.

Chapter 4

More About My Journey - The Mission

Bloating in happiness, bleeding in love,
exploding in gratitude, overjoyed with fun illusions of life.

Talking about liquid prosperity and health success is my personal story, from my own skin and heart. I have tried not to be personal here, but it is almost impossible. I am what I am today because of my relationship with water. In the past, I did everything society expected me to do and to be. But in the end, I found success in the premium liquid of life. These words have nothing to do with money, but with finding peace, happiness, enjoyment, love, and gratitude every day of my life.

Once, I was like everybody else. I was employed at prestigious companies and experiencing what usually society means by "success". I was "prosperous" economically, enjoying social activities, dressed up in high heels, expensive clothes, fashion accessories, and perfect makeup. I lived the "perfect way of life", as many other people have done. And I did it long enough to learn from the experience and to value my personal beliefs.

The jobs I had, combined with raising three children, one with special needs, and facing a complicated divorce, was a bit much to handle for quite a long time. Everything in life comes to a point where you must consider its functionality or utility. In my case, the job -and everything I was facing- worked against my health and quality of life, not only because of what I was doing, but because of what it represented regarding my own values.

I found myself dedicating my working hours to promoting unhealthy products and companies. I had a personal campaign against alcohol, but I was working for a distributor of alcoholic beverages. I needed the income, and that was the job I found just as I was getting divorced. I have also hated smoking habits throughout my life. Yet, I was offered a great promotion, one I desperately wanted at that moment, and accepted to work for a tobacco distribution company, even when I was completely against smoking!

Being forced to overlook your own values and morals to ensure your survival and economic situation creates a lot of stress, which translates into a lot of body ailments. It got to a point where I decided that enough was enough. I reached a dramatic crossroad in my life, and decided I needed to head in a new direction.

In that process, I sought relief in Hata Yoga, in meditation, and in the ocean. They helped me maintain my stability and mental health, and they helped me see all the paths that become available when you look for them. I talked to my co-workers about creating a new future with yoga, water, and rehabilitation. I visualized it. I was certain of my dream, starting with my own personal commitment to a healthy lifestyle.

Long story short, I traded the high heels for being barefoot; the business suit was replaced by fashion bathing suits; fancy pants and skirts were substituted by a sarong, and, only sometimes, by rash guards. My office is now a swimming pool, my ceiling is the sky, my titles are liquid, and my steps are always ascending. My music are the birds and the wind chimes. The wind and the pool are now my engines. My boss is God and my staff are my guardian angels and life beings. The aromas I breathe are natural from the trees around me. The staff meetings are held during my personal lunch time, with friends and clients. Weekend conventions are limited to my personal paintings and beach time. Special trainings are special retreats. I take free time to relax, read, laugh, meditate. I communicate with compassion in a sensory way while connecting with my clients. I have a liquid and prosperous life, with all the ingredients of a very healthy lifestyle. I love giving water sessions, being floated, and have fun in the water. I am very me, very simple and basic. I no longer require most of the material things I thought I needed before this stage of my life. I feel like a five-year-old with a license to play, explore, and be free.

I believe in happy conclusions, and my life is full of them, but believe me, it is not perfect. Following your heart, facing the unknown and messy road of entrepreneurship, and delving into a respected field that is unknown in your marketplace, all that was messy and frustrating. Going from pool to pool, some good but not appropriate for therapy, pushed me to build my own state-of-the-art facility, supported by Dr. Igor Burdenko.

But when life is driven by a mission, all the pieces fall into place in unexpected ways.

Once I started on my mission and began giving water therapies, everything started to flow like water - transparent, lean, clean, refreshing. Everything bloomed. Everything began feeling, tasting, looking, and sounding amazingly happy. I am not saying I was not scared, I was. I risked everything, but the call was stronger and the risk worth taking.

When things appear to get complicated, there is always a new perspective or a lesson to be learned. Pain is a polarity we all need to experience, but suffering is not required. How I embraced and managed pain and sorrow became the key to my own evolution. The clue is to understand where pain comes from, how we are partly responsible for it, and how we can turn it into purpose. In my case, my own success!

The best gift I have in my life is that I am the best version of me, with no pretension, no masquerades or disguises to please a CEO, colleagues, or anyone else. The only person I need to impress is me and my conscience. This is the legacy I am leaving to the next generation and to my children, with my actions as an example. This is my simple liquid prosperity story.

The intention behind sharing all the stories in this book is to share health success, based on the combination of protocols of different alternative aquatic modalities that have transformed lives. Water is within us, and it is the way we replicate love since birth, in everything we do, think, behave, and relate to every day, in every appreciation or form of life.

You will comprehend this book when you see how success in health goes beyond one method, symptom, or medication. A smart investment in rehabilitation time and personal commitment to healing are the keys to health success.

In the end, it's just a matter of working to achieve anatomical integration with mental and spiritual synergy.

Chapter 5

Hitting the Blue Wall

Broadening the horizons of your dreams,
unarmed but uneasy, just move the wall.

I have never thought of my practice as a career, but rather a mission.

I remember working with a person during the early days of my practice that absorbed my full attention, even when I was not working. The person was so afraid and dependent on me that, in trying to help her, I felt I was pushing against a concrete wall. All along, I could not read that she really had no intention of getting better.

I was so eager to help other people, that I invested even my personal time thinking about clients and other ways to help them overcome their own process. This was very harmful to me. I felt so committed, because I had gone through a process myself, that I wanted everybody to heal and feel as good as I felt with my body. I wanted the world to feel as safe and connected to their bodies as I felt. I love water so badly, I wanted to invite everyone to get in it, and deeply. I was an empath, innocent, naïve and childish. Now it's hilarious, but at that moment, it was dangerous!

One night, while going through this ordeal, I dreamt that I was literally moving an ocean-blue, solid concrete wall. I felt the pain of pushing all that weight. The sweat, the paralysis I felt, the frustration of it all. The dream was physically and mentally exhausting.

The blue wall became a symbol for a reality check. In my case, a reality check about my position as a therapist. And for any of us, a reality check about our true mission in life.

In terms of therapy, I have hit that reality check wall a few times. These were times before I discovered the treasure of being a resource for the body. I was suffering the healing syndrome, what I call "the ego wanting to control".

Consciously, I knew I was trained to stay in a neutral space, professionally speaking. It was not my task to move anything. I was just a resource to help the body. I finally understood and detached myself from the wrong idea that I could heal everybody. I felt I needed a transference away from the typical empath that I was. I had to develop healthier barriers as a therapist. This also helped me create other boundaries in my personal life.

I do not have healing power in my hands or touch, as many people claim. I believe there is energy working through me, but it is no magic. It is just a technique with the direct intention of assisting the body. I am just there, present, connected, and neutral, so the client can manifest to me what I need to follow. I believe in energy work and the power some people have. In the water, I think it is different. Water is the master working through the person's tissue. I am just there to allow what must happen.

I remember a client who was coming in for a long craniosacral therapy. She would get very distracted, and she experienced strong somatic emotional releases. She moved in the water as if she were having very strong seizures. They were so strong that I had to instruct her to try to control her movements so she wouldn't hurt herself. They got worse every day, and she would scream out of control. She claimed she was going through a very hard time, suffering from general pain, especially headaches. At the end of each session, she felt some relief, but was exhausted and sad.

In the process, she revealed a long history of sexual abuse from her ex-husband, and she felt she had a devil in her body that wanted to get out. But then, the conversations about the man causing her trauma changed from the husband, to the priest, to her uncle when she was a child.

A few sessions later, she had a conversation with our secretary and changed her whole story once again. She did not know reality from fantasy. She later confirmed she was taking schizophrenia medication.

Three sessions were enough to know there was nothing I could do to help her. This was the moment I stepped aside and opened the door for her to get another type of therapy. Everything we had talked about in our forty-five-minute evaluation interview was not real at all. Her reality was only in her mind, and she believed it.

The blue wall dream has been one of my best allies to stop doing more than I should and allow beautiful things to happen. When it presents itself to me in the water, there is always an amazing way to just climb over it, and keep investing in clients that truly deserve precious time and love for their commitment to trying to evolve. It opened my eyes to my right to say "no" to treating certain clients. It empowered me to decide the treatment and the conditions and accountability of both parties before starting a therapy process. Now, I emphasize grounding and protecting the space between client and therapist by doing a thorough initial interview with different techniques to validate where the client really is, regarding his or her healing process.

The blue wall presents itself very fast, in a big way. But once you recognize it, you can see its beauty in a cool way. In the end, it offers a very good lesson that allows you to elevate beautifully to new heights.

Chapter 6

Sixty Letters... With Love

One last personal note

When I was turning forty, I was in the middle of big changes and turmoil in my life. As I mentioned before, I was unhappily married, my children were small, and I had a calling to do much more with my life. I needed to honor my talents and skills to elevate my game. I am unique and full of myself when I feel the need to take charge of my circumstances, to move forward and thrive, no matter what. Creativity is one skill that sometimes scares me.

So, I began the process of doing something truly good with my life. I was considering creating something that would make me feel complete. I was empowering myself, planning to develop the first institution of aquatic therapy that could offer services for handicapped children in the area. I had two objectives: provide therapy for my son locally, and provide it for other children as well. This was a full commitment to the cause of special children.

The opportunity was there for the taking. At first, my husband and I were considering opening an aquatic center after exploring a hospital that offered such services. We talked about it, but there were no real grounds for going forward at that time. Our marriage was unstable and a divorce was forthcoming. I wanted to develop the idea, but I knew that the financial factor was going to be a challenging part of my decision. I was very busy with my children, deliberating when and how we were going to solve our situation.

The turbulent airwaves I was flying at home were scary and threatening. That was part of the process. My life was full of uncertainty in terms of what was going to happen in the future. I felt there was something good inside of me, even when I could not see it clearly then.

In the middle of this turbulence, I decided to fly in a different direction with a positive attitude. I must admit I was perhaps a little bit driven by my own fantasy world, but I discovered during this time that you can be happy within yourself, regardless of the circumstances you might be going through.

The way each person deals with chaos is unique. Mine was creative. I decided to do an inventory of all my relationships to see what was really on my plate.

I was turning forty, quite a dramatic number for a lot of people. Yet, I looked and felt fabulous. I was free, healthy, and grateful. For me, turning forty was a perfect moment for change and growth. To be honest, I think I have not aged since then. Ok, go ahead and laugh. I also laugh when I say this, but I mean it!

The factor that made me grow and separate from the past, was the feeling that I had so much to live for, and my marriage was a setback. The wind of emotional pain was as overwhelming as it was physically hurtful. There were times I felt that I could not breathe. But I also had to accept that marriage was my decision as well, so I had to deal with it. While it was difficult for both my husband and I, separation was the best opportunity for each of us to fly off and succeed on our own.

My gift to myself on my fortieth birthday was sending forty letters to the people I loved at that moment in my life, including my soon to be ex-husband. I bought beautiful stationery and envelopes, and started writing to share with these people why they were special to me. The letters were intended to thank them for their presence in my life, the connection I felt to them and, even if they were not close to me at the time, that I felt blessed to have them in my life.

I had so much fun crafting these letters, being honest and sending these people love. It was a real blast! With this project, I realized that all the memories were not happy ones. Yet, I was certain that I was going to express myself without hurting anybody.

My dolphin intuition started to hit the paper. I would not re-read the letters; I did not want them to be revised or changed. I was speaking from my soul. They were moving letters. Before sending them, I did a personal ritual and a meditation to send them with love, gratitude, and compassion for myself. It was very hard to finish some, especially the one for my husband at the time. Being honest to myself through this writing exercise could bring all kinds of consequences, and I was ready for that.

It's funny how being bold and authentic to yourself could be disastrous to society and to relatives. I sent those letters, uncommitted to any result. At the end of each letter, I asked the person not to talk to me about it. Secondly, I gave clear instructions not to talk to anybody about it and, finally, to destroy the letter after reading it.

My intention was to let them know how I felt, and to thank them for whatever reason life gave us our experience together. I also jokingly told them that the letter would self-destroy when they finished reading it! Unfortunately, although that would have been the optimal situation, I did not have the technology to do it!

And so, the letters were sent. I was now totally exposed to the people I had loved. Sending my soul to these people meant so much to me, and it was scary!

The letters arrived to each of the forty people I limited myself to writing. The best part was how people reacted to my authenticity, even when I told them not to talk about it, not even with me. It was hilarious! Some people called me asking me what was going on with me, or if I was dying. Do you have cancer? Are you sick? Are you planning to commit suicide? These were common questions. I told them to just follow the instructions and simply let them know that I loved them.

Some of them talked to other people who had not received a letter, who in turn asked me why had I sent these letters, and why they had not received one. Others just thanked me for the letter without talking about it.

The worst reaction to the letter, as expected, was from my husband at the time. Even though I did not need to send him that letter, mainly because I had told him everything I had written thousands of times before, he felt insulted and humiliated because of what I wrote. His letter was written on a beautiful notebook, so believe me, it was long.

There was not much to lose by writing to him. The reality was that the marriage was already in ruins. All I did was uncork the bottle to let the genie out. I fully opened the door and the whole process flowed faster than expected.

I could not feel better with myself at this moment of crisis. I was true to myself and I was loving me!

My strategy at the time was to confront the idea that being true to yourself can be hard for people around you. It could be risky for yourself to start a solo journey into whatever you want to do. I have always been authentic, but this experience taught me who was trustworthy in my life, who was there for me unconditionally, who knew me, and who could receive gratitude without expectations.

This exercise was the best thing I could have done because it made me appreciate people in my life in so many ways, even the ones that were getting ready to leave my life. Completing my mission just took a few years after that, and the universe was my perfect ally for success from the moment I put my eyes on the property where I built my clinic.

I am still creative, so I repeated the exercise when I turned sixty; sixty letters and sixty "thank you" cards... with love.

Chapter 7

Intimate Passion for Water

Floating, forgetting what I am, in a second of total lack of gravity,
immersed in pure love, enjoying who I am.

There is an intimate and adorable relationship between water and human tissue that embraces life in the most genuine way of unconditional love. From the most basic form of conception in life, from the environment, from a drop, to the biggest ocean, water gives life and heals!

There is an amazing science-evidenced book about the human connection with water, *The Blue Mind*, by Wallace J. Nichols. I highly recommended it. To quote from the book's description, the author combines "cutting-edge neuroscience with compelling personal stories from top athletes, leading scientists, military veterans, and gifted artists", and he shows "how proximity to water can improve performance, increase calm, diminish anxiety, and increase professional success. *Blue Mind* not only illustrates the crucial importance of our connection to water; it provides a paradigm shifting 'blueprint' for a better life on this Blue Marble we call home."

Get Wet and Heal, however, has no scientific pretension; it is not a technical text nor a professional challenge in any way. It is but a journey of human health transformation through the element of water.

Yet, because aquatic healing is also my business, I do like to keep statistics about my clients and their progress. Since I began offering aquatic therapy sessions, thousands of people have enjoyed the pleasure of healing.

About 60 percent of my clients do not know how to swim. Some swim like dogs and survive the experience, while other patients with back pain are referred by their physicians to come swim. Incredible but true. Under these conditions, how can rehabilitation happen!?

Approximately 65 percent are female and 35 percent male. Of the total population, 35 percent comes with different types of chronic back conditions, from herniated discs and bulges, to pre-surgery, post-surgery trauma, and other ailments. The second group of conditions is autoimmune diseases such as arthritis, osteoarthritis, multiple sclerosis, dystonia, fibromyalgia, etc. (of which 50 percent are women); 18 percent come with muscular and orthopedic conditions, including trauma, scoliosis, bad knees, shoulders, hips, necks, etc. (80 percent are male). The rest mostly suffer neurological conditions: ataxia, strokes, neurodevelopment, ADHD, Noonan's, autism in all its varieties, while others are not diagnosed. Believe me, it is a diverse population.

Nearly 95 percent of clients use at least three medications and supplements. The rest of my clients use at least five to nine maintenance medications for pain, cholesterol, high blood pressure, depression, anxiety, sleeping disorders, diabetes, blood thinners, stomach and digestion problems, and other ailments.

Most people with these patterns also have very poor nutritional habits and minimum activity. In short, they live on a recipe for total deterioration. They just take medications prescribed by their doctor, without even questioning dosage, or an intention to change their behavior.

At KinFloat® Aqua Wellness Center we work to change those patterns. Here are a few testimonials from clients who have been coming for AquaYogi® group therapy for the past eight to ten years:

"AquaYogi has helped me more than any other therapy I've had to minimize my muscle and arthritis pain. I prove it every time I miss a session and have to take medicines for my pain. I've been back to the center for only two days and I'm feeling extremely well... You lift my spirit and I leave the sessions full of energy, ready to face anything! I love you all very much, you are very important in my life."

"AquaYogi has solved the dependency I had on pain killers for my herniated cervical and lumbar discs. I have become another person. With the exercises, my pain is way more tolerable and manageable, and the group offers so much support. It nourishes us in so many ways. I am very grateful for that."

"Last Tuesday I was feeling down for several reasons. The group noticed it right away and gave me so much support and love that I left far better than when I came in. Friendship and loving care, that's what's important."

I feel truly privileged and fortunate to have inspired so many people to take a new road towards a healthy transformation. And I feel completely blessed, mostly because we have been able to create a unique concept of community, support, diversity, and inclusion. These are values we live by every day and honestly share with clients and suppliers. They allow us to provide a safe and pleasant environment, especially in stressful moments such as now, with the inconsistencies and insecurities caused by the Covid-19 pandemic.

Chapter 8

Float in Water

Lingering thoughts of letting go of old beliefs, rules,
people, sending them blessings as far as they can reach in glory,
opening a big space for new, fresh, amazing ones.

Here's my personal favorite acronym for "Float" (provided by an appreciative client): Fine Living On Aquatic Therapy.

The definitions for **float-ed, float-ing, floats** listed in the Thesaurus are:

A. To remain suspended within or on the surface of fluid without sinking.
B. To be suspended in or move through space as if supported by liquid.
C. To move from space to space, especially at random.
D. To move easily or lightly.

Floating experiences are defined by the moment, by the instance of living, or the presence of being at one specific but timeless moment of consciousness. It is the moment to just stay still and vividly experience what is happening. It is an occasion to leave time and space, to really see, enjoy, or just forget everything and make a choice to feel and live better.

Floating moments can happen any time of the day in multiple instances. You know you are experiencing them when you feel temporarily disconnected from the current world. You feel your energy elevated to a quantum state, with no definition, while enhancing your perspective about life.

Floating moments are full of who you are, and what you are, with no judgment, mostly an indescribable sensation between body and soul. In your floating moments, you stop having a body and begin experiencing time, form, or mass. You connect with the universe and everything happens without effort on the part of the therapist.

Sometimes, you cannot even tell if it was real or not, but time stops, leaving you with a helium-like sensation of magical internal harmony. Floating takes you to an unprecedented and profound state of meditation that is hard to achieve on land. It transforms the way you see life.

The experience in the water is related to any of the five senses of the body, but there are times when it goes beyond them. Through the eyes, we might experience a glance, a blink, and that is all you need to know in a given situation. But we can see more than what our eyes can see. We see through things, receiving all the knowledge to determine what is real or what is not.

The same happens with touch. Even not touching can give you sensations and information through perfect energy, transpiring in universal knowledge and flawless evidence of what **is**.

Hearing or not hearing is the same. As the Dalai Lama stated on being, "You have to stop being to really be." Being is not a thinking process, but the experience of full pure wisdom.

Floating moments are those where your life seems to stop for a second. Those moments sometimes feel like a transitional stage, when something important will happen and will change the course of your life. Other moments, you feel the need to fly over some situation to successfully continue the journey, no matter how it evolves.

Floating moments happen without discrimination; they come to prove your mastery and faith, as well as your trust in the big plan. Sharing those moments can open the life and perspective of someone with the courage and will to confront his/her reality and move on.

My very personal floating moments have increased my love for life, challenged my persistence, developed my intuition, and made me as unique as I am. The bottom line is a "love me first" sensation that is necessary to transcend any circumstance.

Likewise, a floating moment can change all the predicaments of the past, even change genetics, predispositions, and everything that is socially expected to be.

Nothing is real, and reality is just a present moment of beauty and trust. Reality is not just what we imagine and accept, it is also the physical and scientifically proven connection and balance of the nervous system. That's why self-healing is not magic; it is self-regulation, balance and stability transmitted from your brain to your body. Self-healing is evidence-based.

It has been a common belief that our brains deteriorate little by little as we age. However, Dr. Daniel Amen, a psychiatrist and brain disorder specialist, author of multiple books, and director of the Amen Clinics, has studied thousands of brain conditions using SPECT imaging. He has proven that we can improve our brains, that "we are not stuck with the brain we have", as he puts it.

Now, science is pointing to how the brain can change, regrow, and be enhanced with better choices. Many other specialists agree with Dr. Amen on these findings, which are changing the paradigms of preventable mental illness and the way to live more fulfilling lives.

It has also been proven how meditation and self-connection can have a substantial healing effect on the body and mind, because the brain is involved in everything we do and relate to, how we think and behave. We need to be in touch and in love with it. As Dr. Amen says, "fall in love with your brain, and everything will be better."

To sum it all up, as a Brain Revolution coach, I can say that you are not stuck with the reality you have created because it is your responsibility to take charge of your life and live it fully.

Recognizing a floating moment is challenging and mysterious. The more one embraces the lessons, the better the learning experiences. In his book *Illusions*, a classic and beautiful text, Richard Bach describes "...the way life is and what every moment represents for the producer, the actor, and the theater manager. Since we are all of them in our lives, the plot, the images and the situations, are created and accepted only by us. The ultimate vision of life is an illusion; it is magic and the secret of it is in our control, nobody else's."

Indeed, it is an amazing way to describe this process. In the end, it is a perfect present moment, full of the divine energy that we all have the right to have and be. Enjoy the ride, recognizing these as your personal floating moments. Everybody has their own created story.

I can forecast that the scientific success of water, aside from the lack of gravity, is simply the time taken away from daily routines and chores to just be with no pretension, in absolute meditative moment with yourself. Dedicating time and space to yourself is like boarding a special capsule of perfect gravity, freedom, and safety. It is a moment you own and treasure, giving total attention to your body and mind. It is time to hear your body language and feel membranes adjusting to the balance and synergy of your body, soul and mind.

Chapter 9

Water Fusion

Water keeps surprising me with happy conclusions and lots of LOVE!

Biological tissue, as it will be referred to from now on, is the term to describe a cellular organizational level that does not comprise a complete organism. Hence, a tissue is an ensemble of cells, not necessarily identical, but from the same origin, that together carry out a specific function. This functional grouping of multiple tissues is what we call organs.

As it relates to aquatic therapy, we will be talking about muscle tissue, skin tissue, organ tissue, and everything we can feel in the water. Tissue has an individual behavior, form, temperature, movement, texture, and other features. The way it behaves gives us therapists information about healthiness, inflammation, pain, release, pathology, and other issues. All this information is received from senses such as touch, sight, hearing, and smell. It may sound weird, but it is not. In the water, when the tissue is not defensive, you can feel a lot. For example, the same odor from people with the same condition and taking the same medication, can be identified in the water, especially from their breath.

The quality of the tissue can also allow you to access the lymph nodes, which are mostly responsible for protecting the body's immune system. Everything in the body is entwined in a cohesive mode, in perfect function. This perfection is so amazing that, with an accommodating opposition, pressure or flow, you can change the behavior of specific areas, enhancing their function for the better.

During the Covid-19 pandemic, we saw many clients with overactive immune systems causing inflammation of the joints, under the arms, and the inguinal region. Some experienced pain due to either the virus itself or the inoculation. Tissue manipulation under water helped these clients through their healing process.

The bottom line is that the tissue talks to us therapists through the water, melding with it, allowing things to happen. When I do this, I feel like I am just flying over an area, like a kite, allowing the winds to take my hands where they are needed.

When working in the water, there are times when the tissue seems to lose its solid state and starts fusing with the wet environment. That is the most exhilarating sensation. It means the tissue is not fighting or resisting any more. Just like ice, it melts in water slowly but surely, allowing the water to facilitate the job.

You can also imagine a melding effect in the tissue. The melding idea teaches you to just let things happen during therapy. When you are melding a piece of metal, you do not need to use more force, you just need to heat it more. This was an important learning process for me. Even though I know water blends with the tissue naturally, allowing the melding to happen is key in the healing dynamic. When melding occurs, blending and synergy also happen. At that point, as a therapist, I feel I have a license to get in, to explore, and allow great things to flow.

Sometimes, instead of blending, the tissue builds up, letting you know it is not ready for a certain therapy. This happens a lot while applying craniosacral therapy in the water, my favorite therapy modality.

The tissue behaves on its own, according to the energy in the body. Once the tissue lets go of resistance, with some guidance, you can even feel and imagine the spread and relaxation of the fascia (the thin casing of connective tissue that surrounds and holds every organ, blood vessel, bone, nerve fiber, and muscle in place). It is so exiting! I picture the fascia as a packed cotton candy ball. When you put a piece of cotton candy in your mouth, you feel the tingling sensation of the sugar mixing with the saliva. It is a fun sensation.

Isn't it amazing how nature works so perfectly and miraculously, while transforming matter so easily!

During my journey in the water, my hands fly over the tissue, experiencing major reactions in the way it responds to different techniques and different media. It's the she same way the body reacts to different medications and different approaches amongst the variety of medical and scientific alternatives in the world to treat the same condition. For some people, invasive approaches in situations such as trauma or catastrophic injury is the perfect solution. Here, science pushes and pulls the strings of knowledge to save the person as it unveils stored trauma. The difference is the intention of the administrator and the belief from the receiver.

In the process, the best technique is just to move the strings of the client's tissue in such a way that, at the end of the session, the restrictions are loosened. The freedom of the untangled strings of the tissue allows the body to relax, to move freely and surprisingly gracefully.

Tissue does not lie. And clients do not lie intentionally either, of course. Sometimes they just assume that what the physician diagnoses is what it is and accept it. But then the tissue says, "this is not what it is!" Other times, there is nothing wrong with the body, but the tissue says there is an unconscious symptom causing pain.

I had a case of a lady in her forties who was going through a very bad relationship. I knew this beforehand, but I do not get into a client's personal matters, unless it is prudent to do so, or the client opens that door and it's relevant to his or her case.

The lady came in with neck and shoulder pain after a bike fall. "Piece of cake!" I thought. During therapy, she expressed frustration about suffering pain for almost a year, and having gone through lots of physical therapies and several physicians. She was a young, active, and healthy professional, so the best treatment for her was Bio-Aquatic therapy, combined with Watsu®, followed by exercises.

During the first stage, even though there was great improvement in releasing the tissue, I felt there was something else. She was satisfied with the results and began exercising. During therapy, she would have strong somatic emotional releases. It was clear that the shoulder was fine, but there were other issues that did not allow the neck to heal.

We continued with the exercises, she kept strengthening her shoulder and was doing great. But symptoms like insomnia and anxiety were still giving her trouble. For almost six month, she kept doing great, but suddenly she stopped coming to her sessions. "Great!" I thought. Perhaps she went on with her running and biking, so it was a success story.

Not so. We received a call from her sister saying she was doing very badly, with chronic thyroid problems, as well as bacteria in her stomach. She was bedridden, could not work, and she was going through a battery of nuclear tests. Worried, we followed up. Months passed and she did not improve, even losing thirty to forty pounds. She was depressed and almost suicidal.

In a very subtle way, she trusted me a lot, and called me. She wanted to lower her anxiety and stress, so we did some meditation and therapeutic yoga. I was very busy and could not dedicate her the time she needed, so I referred her to a psychology and meditation teacher in my own facilities. She continued with health issues and getting worse.

One day, after a Bio Aquatic therapy, she had a very strong somatic emotional release. Due to guilt, embarrassment, and anger because she was disappointed with her progress, she burst into tears, full of rage against herself. Everything opened like a memory box. She flipped open the top and started exposing all the fear and terror in her relationship. The tissue released all her feelings in a wonderful way, opening the door to real healing. That was the perfect example of how tissue talks and gets in contact with the nervous system instantly. She continued with psychological support and she is doing great!

A similar case is that of another lady in her early forties from Atlanta. Alice (not her real name) came recommended by her aunt, who is one of my clients, and happens to be a physician who experienced the blessing of alternative aquatic therapy at my center.

Alice had been treated by neurologists, anesthesiologists, and physiatrists, regarding an excruciating pain she had been suffering for seven years on the left upper quadrant of her back, and was now irradiating to her chest.

She was a teaching dean at a well-known college, and the pain was affecting her personal and professional life. The pain was so strong, she would often fall to the floor, or would have to sit down to endure it. She was married with two children, but felt incapacitated with depression and panic attacks.

Attempting to at least manage her stress and pain, Alice signed up for three sessions. She would cry and scream every time she felt the pain. In the water, the pain increased when I did visceral manipulation or cranial work over her spleen.

Because she was a teacher, I asked her to write down every night whatever emotions had come along with the pain during therapy, without judging them. She did her writing exercise and came in for a fourth session. It was then when she started to recognize she was feeling shame and guilt without knowing why.

The fifth session was glorious and strong. During therapy, she felt scared and saw herself when she was seven years old, in a dark room and in the presence of someone that made her feel paralyzed. The pain began to subdue a bit after this vision.

I told her to remember that, regardless of what she had experienced in the past, she was now an adult and a powerful woman. That night, while in pain, she realized that the vision she had of the dark room was at her grandfather's home. Soon, the pain started to ease down and she was able to sleep. Writing down her emotions was crucial in the process of expressing her sensations of pain.

On her sixth visit, she cried like a baby. But her sorrow was different. Suddenly, she was quiet, calm, and relieved. She did not say a word during the rest of the therapy.

At the end of her session, she opened up and told me she had the vision about her grandfather's house again, and she felt sad and scared. That night she woke up and remembered everything. She was molested by her grandfather's best friend, while her mother went to work the night shift at the hospital. He would touch her and tell her that if she screamed, he would also do it to her four-year-old sister on the other bed.

It was a blocked trauma which healed at that moment. From that point on, her life bloomed. She solved her own puzzle, not me. The memory of the tissue and the nervous system erased her fear and freed her from a highly toxic trauma that she had endured since she was seven years old.

Again, it is all a matter of moving the strings of the tissue in such a way that the restrictions of the body are loosened. The untangled strings of the tissue let the body relax, feel free and graceful.

Chapter 10

Wet Tissue Language

Working in the water, I have learned things about physical tissue that no one had taught me before. I discovered how different the tissue feels in the water as compared to how it feels on land; how tissue can be affected by touch; or how to identify if the tissue has improved. As a land massage therapist, the contact with different textures, qualities, sensations, odors, and pains is inevitable, and you get a taste of that during training!

In the water, therapy is a whole different story. When gravity is not present, all the poly dimensions of space and inactivity reveal the unmasked tissue. For me, it has been fascinating to detail and describe how the wet tissue experience provides valuable information.

This is a fascinating part of the alternative aquatic therapy journey. I do a thorough examination, including history, movement, and touching the tissue on land when I see the person for the first time, and during the evaluation process. However, the real assessment occurs in the water.

When I get in the water and start a session, I begin by feeling the reaction of the spine. I then qualify the tissue regarding tone, spasticity, if it's hypotonic or flabby, if there's bloating, and other sensations unique to the unguarded tissue.

It is challenging and incredible to see the progress in muscle quality when doing wet tissue work. But not all physical therapists like doing tissue work. I have asked other aquatic body workers about this experience and I have been told they do not want to do it, even said it making a nasty face. They prefer modalities where they don't have contact with tissue, missing out on the beauty and the profound healing properties of Watsu®, Healing Dance or other similar therapies.

Touching the tissue creates a connection with the story of the body. In craniosacral therapy, you can connect and relate to the tissue, or feel its restrictions by identifying any changes in color, stains, temperature, or texture. Changes may signal inflammation, or other related tissue qualities. You can even connect to the cells and to the immune system. You may receive a privileged communication from them, allowing you to react properly to it, or to stay away from the area. That is why being fully present is the key to knowing when and how to apply a particular therapy.

Temperature and other sensations may also signal restrictions. When the tissue gets in the water, the tissue is unguarded and you may feel bumps, overwork, temperature, elasticity, pain, boils, fiber homogeneity, irregularity, lack of muscle mass, emptiness, any metals or pieces in the body, and total inactivity.

This is not a scientific approach or theory. It is my own personal experience with the tissue, which facilitates the communication with it as I identify its progress. The body itself, without getting into the technical language of the KinAquaFlow® modality, has rhythm and the rhythm can change from one part of the body to another, sending different messages to guide the process.

I tend to imagine every anatomical body as a different kite, with different colors, designs, and directions, and all having their own rhythms and purposes.

Now, let's share the different types of tissues. Some may sound funny, but please don't laugh!

Types of tissue

1. **Flabby, Empty Water Sack** - This is how extreme hypotonic tissue feels due to spine trauma, lack of movement, or loss of muscle mass after surgery or a traumatic injury. Basically, it represents weakness and a depleted tissue. When treating the extremities, sometimes you can touch the bone with no restriction. In the abdominal area, you can feel the intestines or other organs without restriction, feeling there is not even visceral protection, although there is. In the arms and legs, it feels as some sort of leather covering, with no tone or life. I have felt this kind of tissue in cancer patients after chemo and radio therapy, spine trauma, post meningitis quadriplegic, post brain stroke, or simply fibromyalgia patients with an inactive lifestyle, regardless of age. It can be described as an old tissue.

   This kind of tissue can change in a short time when alternative aquatic therapy is done at least four times a week and resistance is applied without hurting the joints. The muscle begins to gain mass and, if properly fed with oxygen during sessions, the muscle starts to show its beauty. The amazing thing with this type of tissue is that it improves its movement and strength, while body energy improves as well.

2. **Sand Bag with Sand** - This kind of muscle tissue feels as if it were disconnected from the bone. It feels amorphous and empty. The tissue moves without resistance. It is found in patients over fifty with no muscle condition, people with weak bones, and in congenital hypotonic babies. This kind of muscle needs a lot of movement and exercise. Swimming is a great discipline for improving strength. This tissue improves very slowly and takes more time than others. When it fills up, it feels like a soft cloth cushion. In some cases, this tissue may be lost as fast as it is gained, which creates the need for constant exercise for a long period of time.

3. **Jellybean Bag, Full of Beans** – This tissue is not flabby, since it has some tone and is covered by fat. It is not detected immediately; you have to feel the jellybean bag inside the tissue. This is specially found in fibromyalgia patients, inactive adults in their thirties and forties and older; people with no history of physical condition at all; people with poor

diets and low self-esteem; mostly in women. This tissue requires resistance work and a lot of lymphatic drainage. Normally, these clients retain a lot of toxins and liquids, have a low metabolism, and are taking at least three medications, including anti-depressives and cortisone. Usually, metabolic syndromes are found in these clients. When the condition improves, the person may complain about not losing weight, but his/her clothes fit better. Recovery is relatively fast if a nutritional program is followed to help detoxify.

4. **Packed Bed Mattress with Reinforcement** – This is how a hyper tone tissue that has long suffered from spasms feels like. It feels as if it had tension bars behind it. It can be found in bodies packed with toxins and liquid, which do not allow any space for movement or even pain. It is tissue so stiff, that even taking anti-inflammatory and relaxant drugs, or receiving land massage, aromatherapy, acupuncture or a chiropractic alignment, would never get released. It feels like it wants to explode That is why it's so awesome to work this tissue and see how it starts to get tender, with some pain at first, but finally released and relaxed, feeling adequate for normal movement.

5. **The Wall** – It is common in bodies with the highest levels of spasticity due to spine trauma, or cerebral/neural dysfunction. Occasionally, it is found in Parkinson's, cerebral palsy, multiple sclerosis, and muscular dystrophy patients. This is a very hard tissue and very difficult to work with, especially if there is mental stubbornness that doesn't help the healing process. The good thing is that it may fight at the beginning, but water will win, giving it flexibility, elasticity, and better function.

6. **The Tube** – It is often found in patients with autoimmune diseases, when levels of mental spasticity lock the pain in the body and limit movement. The muscles feel as if they were wrapped in a compact tube, like the wires in a high-voltage electric cable wrapped in insulation. When the tissue starts to improve, it seems as if the insulation wrapping begins to thin out, and you can start feeling the muscle fiber. The person moves with difficulty and pain, but gradually improves and feels like new again.

7. **Overcooked Potato Skin** - This tissue can be described as wrinkled flesh, empty of muscle mass. You can feel the bone structure under the skin, especially when treating arms, hands, and feet. The rest of the body is full of flesh filled with gel. It is characteristic mostly in inactive older people over seventy, but it is also common after bariatric surgeries, or severe weight loss not followed by an exercise program.

Enjoying movement without pain goes beyond personal satisfaction for the receiver. Releasing the body from restrictions is a wonderful and liberating sensation. As a facilitator, watching this process of wellbeing is exciting, but for client and therapist alike, it is truly an "aha!" moment.

Let's float with this perception of the tissue. Let's just have fun with the quality of tissue! You can laugh or learn. It's your choice!

Chapter 11

Aquatic Body Talk

Immersed in a typhoon, circling without space or matter, waiting for the moment of released light and life, only in water.

Tissue in the water speaks loudly and clearly. Yes, the body talks in the water more than people think.

When I evaluate a client at the beginning of the process, I always conclude that land evaluation is limited, based on what I have learned during training. I have revised this evaluation process a few times, improving it by adding several questions. But it is not until you go in the water that you get the correct unconscious information from the client's body. And, as part of our therapies, we include basic movements to measure ROM (range of motion) and torsions, and to measure pain as well. The body talks, and loudly, believe me.

You don't even get half of the story until the person goes in the water. If a client said he or she came for this or that pain, once they get in the water, other parts of the body express themselves and can even confuse the person experiencing the process. This is so, especially when a person is used to denying reality and never looks inside him or herself. It is incredible how everything blooms without forcing it.

I have studied many land therapies that I can apply in the water. Based on different modalities and theories, the body screams easier in water. It may resist for the first ten to fifteen minutes of therapy, but then it starts to loosen up. Again, lack of gravity does not allow the body to lie. The best thing to do is to not rationalize it; it will come out by itself. Then, the client begins to discover things about his/her body he/she had not felt or seen before. The way people move their hands, spine, legs, the way the body contracts, folds, spreads, flexes, turns, all have the objective of fixing something through the multi-dimension of water.

The other thing that water does is change the body into a beautiful and perfect one. Each body in the water has beauty. The contractions, releases, and decompression, leave the body in a smooth, flowing, sensual, glorious self.

God made perfection simple. When a cerebral palsy child starts to move in the water, releasing his/her body naturally, grace and freedom blossom. When back pain is relieved, the body comes back in a sleekly moving way. When neck pain eases, the arms and body move in dancing rhythms of happiness. The body in the water expresses all that, and more.

When a body enters the water, it assumes a natural position, what we call the body's intrinsic movement, which is based on the body's current state or condition. In my practice, I use this natural positioning of the body in the water to determine a course of action for that client. This is a very personal, unique, and creative way of interacting with the body in silence. This is not intended to be a theory or a dogma, but rather practical experience.

I love this body talk, and welcoming this language facilitates my work and my communication with the tissue. It fascinates me. I usually envision the human body in a very simple way. I see it as a matchstick figure. That simplicity allows me to understand more clearly changes of posture and the mechanical function of the entire body.

Here are some of the common traits and body positions I have observed during therapy:

1. **The Scarecrow Position -** Just imagine it. It screams loudly: "I am scared!" The arms are extended stiffly at shoulder level, elbows straight, and the wrists are bent inwards like a scarecrow. This happens during a stroke, leaving a scary sensation of needing protection and being out of breath, waiting to be released from the pain. Spasticity in the neck and brachial area is intense. Even if the person wants a release, the brain does not. Legs may be relaxed but mostly they are tightly close to each other. The battle between the nervous system and the soul is intense. When the release comes, the arms and wrists relax and fall softly to the side of the hips. Legs open out, allowing some movement at the hip. I usually see this position in patients with severe Multiple Sclerosis (MS), cerebral palsy, Gillian-Barre, stroke, and ataxia.

2. **Anatomy Posture -** In this posture, the core (middle part of the body) is still, the legs are open and straight, and so are the arms. The message from this posture is that the body expects a change from the outside without the person making a commitment to improve his or her life. It is another way of saying "I am not flexible"; "I do not trust you yet"; "I am waiting for you to do something magic for me"; "What am I doing here?" When the body starts to release, normally the arms relax before the legs. Jerkiness may happen in the whole body, especially in the core (middle part of the body), and the legs start to react. Most of these cases are people with a very tense body: athletes, or hyperactive personalities, people afraid of the water, or who are trying too hard to float.

3. **The Stick -** The body is like a toothpick with pointing legs, arms stuck to the hips, as if the person were constantly protecting him or herself. Sometimes the person is afraid of water, afraid of moving, and seemingly paralyzed. The spine is not free, nor is the rest of the body. The head is sunk into the clavicles, leaving no space to work the neck. Muscle tension is high, and there is constant fear. They do not even trust themselves. They trusted doctors and medication that have not worked, and now they ask: "What can water do that medical therapy could not?" When the body releases, the legs start

to move shyly. By the second or third session, they want to dance extravagantly in the multi-dimension of water. Sometimes tremors and a fever-like sensation manifest before releasing, but then, voilà! all is fine and well. This kind of client takes more sessions to release than others. The stick position has been related to people who have been in a coma, quadriplegics, people who suffer from fibromyalgia, who have had severe spine stenosis, post-cardiac arrest, post-traumatic disorder, post-back surgery, and even normal people who are just afraid of water.

4. **The N Body** - It is a body in pain. The head is resting on the floating device, or the therapist's hands or arm, but the sacrum is very low in the water, crunching the abdomen, and the knees are bent at 15 grades, forming an N. It signals lack of trust being in the water, not trusting the therapist, or suffering severe low back pain. The message is: "I am not feeling comfortable in the prone (floating face up) position" or "I don't trust my back, it might hurt if it's straightened." This happens a lot with children and adults who are afraid of water, autistic children, people with ADHD and neck pain. Normally, visceral mobilization and sacrum release helps a lot with this position. It takes several sessions to help them trust and release.

5. **Fetal Position -** It is the most trusting position in the water. The person floats sideways in a crouched position. When the spine arches inward, it facilitates solving lots of issues. It happens when the person is releasing birth issues, or simply accommodates to release spine restrictions. The arching demonstrates a lot of trust, assertiveness, and spine flexibility. The person does not care what others may say or think. Going inwards demonstrates the person is not afraid of looking inside. Mostly, they trust the process and feel comfortable in their body. Flexibility is required to achieve this position. It offers a liberating sensation, especially when getting in contact with the inner child and the sensation of being in the womb. When this position is released, you can feel the openness of heart and readiness to confront the world with passion and happiness. During all my sessions, I test the body release and flexibility by this position, when the body is no longer guarding or protecting itself. You can see the fetal position in almost every person who achieves flexibility, no matter their condition, and in people who have acceptance, trust, and no pain. It also happens at the end of a session, especially in underwater sessions, or when the client makes a connection back to being in the womb.

6. **Back Bend** - This is almost an acrobatic position, like the bridge in Yoga, which not everybody can achieve on land, and very few in the water. Some people with neurological conditions have expressed that their the body is calling for a stretch. Others convey that they want to escape the pain in their bodies. It also happens when someone wants to reverse or rectify a posture or position they had developed for a long time. People who work constantly on a computer, for instance, develop shoulder and neck issues. This position can be seen in people who have spine restrictions, dystonia, ataxia, back spasms, and visceral restrictions. The stretch releases the fascia.

7. **The Vortex** - This is the most exciting position. It happens when someone wants to spin their head 180 degrees. That feels awesome! You feel the person's body completely flexible and their neck as elastic as can be. The person turns sideways in a fetal position, at times twisting almost completely underwater, while the head stays sideways on top of the water. These are people with great confidence in the water and in their body. They feel they do not control the movement; it just happens when the body releases from the neck all the way down to the coccyx.

8. **The Fast Kick** - Here, the person's body starts to move in different directions and they make big walking movements, opening and closing their legs and arms softly or fast. They seem to be jogging or dancing, making erratic or beautiful movements. The body is happy, the person feels free and sensuous, active and lovable. Sometimes, the person is just reacting to the lack of gravity when floating. When a person does not feel grounded on land, he or she may feel lost in space. After some time, the movement stops in a blissfully soft and gracious flow, or the person just lets go and rests, stopping the rhythm. It happens when someone has spent a lot of time without moving their legs due to an accident, a trauma, or a lumbar herniated disc. It is common among coma patients, persons with chronic lumbar pain and restrictions, children with cerebral palsy, or people with cardiac issues. It represents freedom of movement and always is a happy response. Once they start to move, they cannot stop. When the release happens, the body relaxes with total bliss. It can also be a response to the insecurity they feel getting in the water and having no control of themselves due to certain conditions. They start kicking in desperation, feeling that that movement can keep them afloat.

Aside from the different messages the body expresses in the water, the different positions also have everything to do with balance of energy. When the tissue is relaxed, and has no energy blocks, the body can show its *Kundalini* energy –the ultimate life force energy; the source of our creative and spiritual powers- in the most gracious way. When this happens, the body designs itself as a wonderful piece of art. At the end, all bodies start looking younger, freer, and happier through movement. Nothing can get better than that.

If we took a picture of a client at the beginning of the therapy process, we would see a sad, stray, torn, and harsh face full of pain, a face of frustration. With therapies, the face changes to reveal a supple and happy expression of contentment, and of release from pain.

The same thing happens with the way the body moves in the water. It starts tight and inflexible. But with aquatic therapy, the body expresses gratitude, flexibility and grace. At that point, the body may feel like a free kite, just enjoying a pleasurable journey of beauty and love.

Chapter 12

Body Jokers

Amazed by the universal orchestra! Rhythms and flow is all it takes!

When you are traveling in pain and with a variety of symptoms, I call those body sensations the **body jokers**.

When pain first appears in the body, you begin thinking it is probably nothing, unless it becomes incapacitating or it affects your daily life. If the pain is not very dramatic, you do not want to accept it, you do not believe in it at first. You look at it as a joker who comes sporadically to play or tell you a joke, not a funny one, but one you can ignore for a while. These jokers never arrive when expected.

Suddenly, the pain you were ignoring for the sake of your peace of mind now shows up in an insolent way, with the intention of shrewdly interrupting your busy schedule.

It appears in an informal and unannounced manner, becoming annoying and irritating. Yes, of course it's annoying, because you have an established agenda, work to do, big plans for the day, and this pain is misbehaving in your body. Now your attention is scattered, affecting you! At some point, the pain joker, even the simplest one, feels like it is blocking your energy, your space, even your relationships. The pain, at times, is as imprudent as someone blocking your car in a parking lot when you are in a rush, trying to get to an important appointment.

Pain can drive you crazy and even make you doubt your own sanity. This is the way my clients describe their fibromyalgia, lupus, rheumatoid arthritis, herniated discs, ataxia, dystonia, and chronic fatigue pain. Good way to describe it!

For some clients, pain is like a minor clause in a document, such as a legislative bill or a legal contract, that voids or changes its original or intended purpose. As with any document, the client knows his or her right to being and feeling well, and will not accept the agreement as it is being presented. This is how they start a relationship with pain. They begin a negotiation process, looking for their best options amongst the ones being presented. These clients are assertive and are committed to their health in an intelligent way. Some clients might receive pain -a body joker- just as an experience, as a situation waiting to explain this unexpected visit.

When trauma appears in someone's life, pain is an unforeseen, but important and difficulty fact or circumstance. For some, it is the end of everything; for others, it is the beginning of a journey and an evolution. When this happens, when you begin to win the fight against pain, some call it a miracle, a triumph against all odds. But what really happens is that the pain joker is isolated from the psycho-emotional level of the person. This disassociation allows the body and mind to use the old neuroscience concept of neuroplasticity (the capacity of neural path to use new connections to restore function) to successfully transcend the lesson of evolution.

In some traumatic situations, the joker plays the very bad joke of totally depleting the energy field that was already quite drained before the trauma. In this case, the body needs a lot of effort to recover. Just as when a trauma leaves a patient in near death or in a coma, the body uses this rest to recuperate. That is why some people wake up after a long period in a coma as if nothing had happened.

This was the case of Christine (not her real name), a college student studying in the U.S. Two weeks prior to her graduation, she was hit by a car when she was crossing the street. She suffered head and body trauma after landing sixty feet from where she was hit. She was lucky to be close to a recognized neurology hospital, where she received excellent care.

She was in a coma for three months. She had various surgeries, including cranial. She lost all her physical abilities. Once she awoke from her coma, she was brought to Puerto Rico and started aquatic therapy, as well as other multidisciplinary therapies with us.

Timing is critical in these cases. She arrived in a wheel chair, she was on medication for seizures and to protect her from brain damage due to the massive bleeding she suffered from the accident.

She was almost numb at the beginning in terms of pain. Spasticity was intense and she had no filter whatsoever when she communicated. She was a warrior, and her "let's do this" attitude allowed us to build together a great therapy team. In addition, her family was amazingly supportive throughout the whole process.

One day, when she was 60 percent recovered, on her way to therapy using her walker, she overheard some people nagging about the water being cold, and other meaningless complaints. She was insulted by the way this people were referring to their "suffering".

She bluntly spoke out loud and had everybody listening. "You people!" she said, "You want to know what is cold? Ask me, because I'm sure you don't know what it's like being in a coma, hearing everyone chatting around you, laughing, and crying because of my situation. I was freezing to death in the hospital bed, unable to talk. The only thing I wanted to do was scream to have everyone stop talking and warm me up. The same happened in the operating room. Please shut up and do whatever you have to do!"

Her reaction had such an impact that a few clients came to me later and told me that after hearing her story, they would never complain again.

She is a warrior indeed. After losing all her bodily functions, pain was nothing for her. Twelve weeks later, she was walking and, before she ended her program, she wore high heels to the pool and prepared herself to show up at her graduation the following year. She totally recovered, with some memory delay. She goes to the gym, works in advertising, and is leading a fully independent life. For me, a standing ovation is the least she deserves.

People are amazed at survivors of trauma because they think about how they would have reacted under the same circumstances. Survivors of trauma possess certainty about preserving life, they show motivation, and will never let themselves be manipulated by the game of pain, or depression. For these people, there is no pain, and if there is some, the perception is different. They never let the body jokers gain control.

The joker can also be a personality adopted by some as a treasured tool in the game of manipulation. In this game, the joker takes the pain as something useful and entertaining.

These people live their life telling themselves they are attached and committed to pain, and they do so to manipulate others. They are so attached to pain that it is no longer an intruder, it is the master. Everyone around them knows how much they are suffering, and pain is their ally in making everybody do as they wish.

The pain, as the joker, gets all the attention, it dominates, makes the person powerful, driving everybody around them crazy. The pain is almost like a tattoo they wear proudly. It is a whole manipulation technique. When they realize that people do as they say, the husband and children, for instance, then their pain "diminishes". And they just keep repeating this behavior to achieve the life they feel they "deserve".

The pain game is like a card game, where the joker is precisely not the intruder with the least of value, but is the highest-ranking card. These are the scariest clients I have worked with. They are totally innocent in front of family members and they think they can manipulate me too. Not so!

By sharing the patient's experiences, you can easily identify who they are and what they are looking for. Maybe you can relate to some of these cases. This is where grounding is crucial to the therapy process. I evaluate these clients on how much I am going to invest in them, or if I should decide to send them home. Sometimes, they achieve great transformations during the therapy process, but others just try to drain your energy, the same way they do with family members.

Some clients have come to us perusing a hidden agenda. But the truth about what they are really looking for always reveals itself. It may be that they want to get damaging documentation for a long legal process against some physician or citizen they want to harm.

They may be tired of working and are looking to get disability. There are dozens, if not hundreds, of other hidden reasons.

I had a very dramatic case of a fifty-year-old pediatric psychologist, who came to us after two years of failed physical therapies due to a car accident. This case was as dramatic as it was hilarious.

Every time we got her in the water for multi-hands therapy, she went into psycho states of hysteria that, from the onset, we felt were pure distraction and manipulation. Her reactions were so ridiculously exaggerated that they became a running joke at the center. One day, my lovely secretary brought a bottle of holy water from her church and splashed it all over this client when she became "possessed". And my nephew, who was in his early twenties and working as our swimming instructor, would jokingly prepare a cross with sticks while my secretary splashed the holy water on the client!

Despite her behavior, we gave her a second chance. This time she went into an outer-body experience. Again, we could do nothing but wait. We spend almost an hour trying to get her out of the water. She was scaring other clients around, so we started some somatic-emotional release therapy to see what could happen.

Her trances were so dramatic that we talked to her about receiving another type of therapy. She had a mad fit because she felt we were saying that she didn't have a trauma. When we saw that her daughter was feeling uncomfortable with the situation, I convinced her that we never thought she didn't have a trauma.

The next day, I received a call from her asking us for a formal letter to certify to her lawyer how ill she was to win a case in court. We suggested she should see a mental health expert.

These are the dangerous jokers that have affected good medicine. They are the ones that scare the hell out of physicians, even those with the best intentions of following the best understood and generally accepted procedures.

Sometimes we prefer not to treat clients that have jumped from physician to physician, looking for information, and none would do a procedure on them. These clients are scared to death. They are real string holders in the journey of life, succumbing to pity and holding on to see who will fall with them.

One of these string holders was Rosa (not her real name), a distinguished and elegant Latin-American woman in her late sixties. She had scoliosis and was evaluated by an orthopedic surgeon, who established that she needed no surgery whatsoever.

She was referred to our aquatic therapy center to help her deal with her back pain. After three weeks of sessions, she was feeling much better, but she still insisted on getting surgery.

Another three weeks went by, and she was the feeling 80 percent better, the best she had felt in ten years. She was exercising, going to a gym, and having the time of her life. Yet, she insisted on the surgery.

It was then when her orthopedic surgeon compared her original x-rays to the most current ones. He was amazed at the amount of correction and better posture his patient had gained through the alternative aquatic therapy process.

No physician has yet agreed to see her. And despite all her progress and healing, she is still looking for a doctor to perform a surgery that she thinks will solve the little pain she still feels.

The jokers of the body are dangerous, like a high-tension electric cable would be for a kite. They can kill, destroy or just tangle you badly enough to abort the growth process.

I love this subject because it keeps me alert and grounded.

Certainty and acceptance of what love is at all levels will always keep you in perfect sanity.

Chapter 13

Other Sides of Pain

*Following my dreams and supporting others
allows paradise to blossom in this beautiful life!*

Pain has different sides. First, it is an uncomfortable disgusting sensation that you are feeling in some part of your body caused by an injury or a disease. Secondly, pain is a feeling of sorrow, sadness, and self-pity produced by a contrariety of any type. Are we talking about two different things, or are they both the same? The polarity between pain and pleasure can be very similar if you're not conscious of it.

There is no physical pain without an emotional charge. I am expressing this from personal experiences with clients. In chronic conditions like physical pain, there is always some emotional element. And you don't know what started first, the pain or the emotion? It is very hard to disconnect one from the other without the adequate skills. When the brain starts to connect with wellbeing, pain changes its form and function.

Sometimes, a person's personality changes to adapt to the condition of pain. The person thinks he or she is in pain and you can see them as a walking pain. Depressive energy projects itself as a victim with a pathetic attitude towards life. It is interesting how this concept is so simple, yet so complicated, and can affect even the most intelligent and brilliant people.

In the process of rehabilitation, I have seen thousands of people that have forgotten who they really are. They forgot their dreams, talents, gifts, desires; they forgot their own reality. But most importantly, they forgot how powerful they are regarding their own health issues. They adopt the most desperate scarceness of spirituality. When pain blurs reality, people can lose their sanity. The good news is that in desperate situations or crisis, there are always key factors that allow light to reverse the pain.

At KinFloat® Aqua Wellness Center, we start from the wellness point, offering alternatives of empowerment to support whatever amount of wellness is left in a client. We start accepting what is at that moment, deleting all preconceived ideas of what should be. Empowerment starts with personal attitude, and an intimate connection between mind and body to change the situation. Strong desire and courage, blended with intimate compassion, is the key to start the process against pain.

By analyzing and understanding a current situation, by knowing why and how we ended up in this event in life, we are in a better position to make a significant, fast, and assertive change.

To be fair, pain is not really an enemy; it could actually be your best friend in preservation. In trauma cases, pain is a blessing.

I had a trauma case of a young client involved in a serious motocross accident that left him bedridden. For him, pain was a celebration. He would tell me, "Debbie, I have a new pain!" I remember one day when that seventeen-year-old told me candidly, "Even my penis is hurting!" That was amazing! We celebrated every day, every pain. In his situation, pain was the initial awakening of his semi paralyzed body. That is what he did with his pain; he just accepted it with a positive anxiety about what would come next. There was a big reason to celebrate.

A person with pain reflects sadness, drawn face tissue, dark rings under the eyes, even red eyes due to lack of sleep or crying. The lack of sun and physical activity causes skin stains and freckles, which is another sign of sickness. Lips become colorless and the zygomatic face muscle is in a spasm, sober, with no expression, no light. The skin turns gray, transparent and tired. Body posture is poor, languid, with shoulders inward. The head hangs low, the neck is humped, and the person walks slowly, like a zombie. Most feel like a fragile and weary old person. I've had people in the pool eighty-six years old and older that were more alive and energetic than some of the young ones in pain!

For persons in pain, frustration is the language of choice. Anger is the tone of expression when someone tells them it is mental pain. Their attitude towards the process is one of having lost the war. Most of the time, they are overmedicated, especially with anti-depressives and analgesics. They recognize themselves as not being consistent at anything, and depending on medication to put their feelings to sleep.

They feel guilty when they're with family members or their significant others. A vicious circle starts to torture them, thinking they could lose their job if things don't get better. They feel lost. Pain has taken away all their intrinsic value as a human being, leaving the person out of the game. What was it like to feel normal or at least well? The person forgot. What was fun? Who knows? Disassociation from the self is worse than being dead.

This description matches that of a street bum. Yet, many of the people described here have good positions and careers. But in pain, they are literally miserable. The clients with the above symptoms, despite having all the money in the world to live perfect lives, lack health.

I heard once said that, when you are in pain, you die at twenty-five and are buried at seventy-five. That is how pain can kill you long before you're buried. Maybe it's just an expression, but it's real.

Of course, pain does not discriminate and there's where we find spiritual scarcity, which can tear any life, mind, and soul into pieces. I have worked with many disgraced people, especially people that doctors had declared were either lost cases or crazy. At the end of the evaluation, I just tell them how blessed they are to receive the big combo of pain symptoms. But I also assure them that we are going to work together to delete that combo of pain.

Let's look at Sheila's (again, not her real name) case. She is a private clinical psychologist in her late thirties, and teaches at a renowned university in Puerto Rico.

She has everything anyone could ask for: success, youth, beauty, a career, and a loving family. She is now a close friend.

She came to me with a calcified vertebra on her neck, referred by one of the best neurosurgeons around. She came with her husband, who seemed extremely worried and frustrated about her condition. They have a beautiful relationship.

She wore a neck collar and was depressed due to pain, and was instructed not to exercise, drive or do other activities. Desperate and sad, she came crying for help because the last doctor she saw told her that only alternative aquatic therapy would help her with the pain. She decided to follow her doctor's advice.

I was kind of worried about this case, but I studied it and finally had the certainty that her neck would suffer no harm at all, and that good energy could help her improve.

She was open to alternative aquatic therapy and trusted it. We started the process using my method of passive therapy. She started to feel better from day one and I was feeling confident about how she was responding. After the third session, she was a lot more flexible and doing movements she was unable to do a week and a half before.

But during her fifth therapy, she had a shift. She cried in excruciating pain and her shoulders were twisting wildly. I continued applying craniosacral rhythm. Suddenly, the pain stopped and she fell into the most profound calmness. At the end of the session, she was crying of happiness and smiling.

She shared with me that she finally understood where her reaction came from. One day, she was walking with her beloved grandma, when suddenly her grandmother collapsed in her arms after suffering a massive heart attack. She held her grandmother with all her strength so she wouldn't fall and carried her to a chair, but she was already dead.

Her pain came from the memory of holding up her grandmother in her arms when she died. It came from not letting go of that terrible moment. As soon as she realized it, her pain was gone.

She continued her therapies and transitioned for the better. She not only strengthened her upper back and neck, but she closed her office and began doing research. She decided she did not want to practice psychotherapy anymore, since relaxation and passive therapy solved her years-long problem in one second. She healed herself. Now, her success is even bigger and her life has thrived in a beautiful way. Even her husband thanked us for bringing back his wife's soul.

These are my favorite cases. They are so interesting to work with because I can almost see when the zygomatic muscle brakes out in laughter. The first step is to change your client's perspective, letting them know they are not alone. I take this very seriously.

Most clients arrive at my center showing the conditions we just described. At first, they receive a minimum of therapies, either Watsu® modalities or craniosacral therapy. And in a short span, their expressions change, adding new light to their faces.

During the first therapy, which always is a "wow!" session for clients, the body and mind connect in a beautiful way, discovering the self. For a brief time, the body remembers what it's like to feel good, to be in no pain and in an absolute perfect state. As if like magic, the body feels the power of oneness and gratitude.

Feeling the body in a state of pleasure under water is amazing. This perfect sensation helps the body reconnect to life and to pain. The practice of forgetting pain during the sessions and feeling complete again is addictive. Being happy is addictive. That is what gives clients the will to come back and continue the process, to commit for the right reasons of feeling better and getting healthier. Just one session could be enough to convince even the biggest skeptics, but it can scare you away if you are not ready to be with yourself and see the ocean of benefits it can produce.

Loosing gravity has an intense effect not only on the body, but on the nervous system as well. The human body is, on average, 70 percent water, while the brain is 90 percent water. Being such malleable creatures, it is indeed ironic to see how strong we think we are.

This is s a funny story. Sissy (you guessed it! not her real name) is a politician in her forties, leading a hectic and stressful life. She was referred by her mother, who is also an influential woman in government.

Sissy was going through a crisis and needed an emergency session immediately. We made space and received her, along with her entire entourage, as usual.

When we got in the water, she was feeling a lot of rage, anger, and pain. She didn't even say good morning! When I started the therapy, she was so closed I could not even get near her. I'm not talking about getting physically close, I'm talking about her energy levels being off the charts.

Little by little I tried to get her to relax, but there was a barrier I could not break. Finally, after twenty minutes of therapy, she started to let go, relax and release. After forty minutes, she was like a baby, flexible and melting like ice.

After the session ended, it took her ten minutes to open her eyes. Then she stood in front of me, making me feel tiny. I am just 5' 2'' and she is 5' 8"! Full of authority, she told me, "At first, I wanted to slap you in the face, and hard. But then I thought, I came here to feel better voluntarily and you are not the cause of my pain. So, I better relax and heal." Then she smiled and thanked me profusely. She still remembers how she talked to me that day. Now we laugh about it.

She came back for the rest of her treatment. She healed and I have treated both of her children. This story always makes me smile.

Rejecting or fighting against this kind of therapy is a challenge for everyone. In every case, either the tissue stops resisting or the water stops being water. Warm water is hard to reject when the body relaxes and the brain decides not to fight. The fusion of tissue in the water recognizes and allows a perfect disassociation with pain, which produces homeostasis between life and joy. Life acquires a new color with a new lens, a real clean lens, not the pathetic one of pain.

One thing I stress to my clients is having a sense of gratitude, and understanding pain as an extraordinary master who presented itself in disguise to teach us something. I also emphasize seeing pain as the beginning of a new way of managing something in life. If a person does not experience pain, they would not seek a solution to the problem that ails them. They would not give themselves the opportunity to solve their dilemma.

Accepting this concept is not easy for everyone. Challenging a typical thought pattern is so scary, that some would rather quit than try to understand. When it comes to rehabilitation, aside from all the external resources available to help the process, there must be a genuine personal desire to heal.

Once a person begins to leave their pain behind during early treatment, you can see them developing a new face, with a glowing expression, pink cheeks, and an open smile. They start accepting their current pain condition as a temporary one. Commitment and proactivity become the new language. It's not that the pain leaves completely, it's that the relation to pain changes and then is released. With just a few therapies, they feel like experts and want to share their experience -with the best of intentions- and want this process to spread around, thinking of all the people who might benefit of it. Their mood changes and everything around them changes as well.

After a minimum number of sessions, they share with and support newcomers. In the water, women feel amazingly sensual, fluid and flexible. Men feel strong and powerful, with a different sense of sensibility and flexibility. Bodies appreciate the natural process of healing. At this point, people become acquainted with the authority and will power they have over their health.

From this point on, success is assured. Nobody can change this. Understanding the self and recognizing body parts that were never noticed before offers an excellent chance to stop a bad situation from recurring. But if something shows as pain, they are ready to easily delete it. A typical expression I hear from clients is: "I never thought I had so many pain points or parts of my body that I was never conscious of." Just that acceptance is an elevated moment of life.

Here are some comments I've received from clients after their first sessions:

"Why didn't you tell me my intestines were going to have some participation. I have never felt them this way."

"I should have had this before."

"I went through a tunnel of yellow light and then saw a violet light. Suddenly, when I started to release and recover, I felt very cold and had tremors."

"The pain reminded me of old issues I thought I had forgotten."

"The pain reminded me how mad I was with myself, and now I know I have to heal."

"Pain is like entering a freezer, but healing is warm and calming."

"Did I dance in the water? I felt my body was in pure freedom while my joints started to sing."

"How did you move me that way? I would have never been able to do that out of the water."

"Never been so relaxed in my life and I do not even know you."

"I lost all sense of space and time. I got lost, but felt amazingly happy."

"God had a conversation with me and told me not to worry because he will always take care of me."

"For the first time, I felt how my body is wired and connected."

"Where is the pain? What happened?"

"This is the best thing that has ever happened to me."

"I never get a massage because I don't like them. The only time I got one, I was counting the minutes it'd be over. Today, I was afraid it would end. I didn't want it to end!"

"It is so sad when it's over. I want to stay here!"

"This should be everybody's right in life. How come I did not discover this before?"

"You don't know how long it's been since I've been hugged and held like this!"

Sometimes, subtle changes in people can make all the difference. Just keep in mind the following thoughts:

- A positive change of attitude allows the possibility to change everything.
- Just feeling someone on Earth understands the pain confirms that you are not insane, and yes, you can succeed.
- Being able to receive support during the process without being judged is a big relief.
- Being heard is so supportive it can change everything.
- Looking at yourself with compassion can make you fall in love with the self.
- Feeling better can bring you back to your normal activities, which is motivational enough to continue the journey.
- Working less hours until total recovery is achieved stimulates healing and, normally, you can go back to working full-time before expected.
- Sometimes, pain forces you to take time for yourself because you needed it.
- Even feeling like buying new clothes is a great sign.
- Put on makeup, fix your hair, wear the pretty dress. You don't have to cry anymore.
- Enjoy nutrition and stop dieting for the wrong reasons.
- Sometimes you have to let others give you a hand without feeling guilty.
- Assistance equipment, such as wheelchairs, canes and walkers, are temporary items needed while making progress.
- Be assertive about doing what you must do.
- Being responsible with yourself is mandatory before you can be available for others.
- Feel proud of your progress every day, regardless of how small the steps.
- Give yourself all the credit.
- People learn to establish limits with others so they don't abandon the process.
- There is no tolerance for excuses.
- Posture improvements facilitate the body to act accordingly.
- Stop unnecessary medication. Allow the body to heal itself.
- Sometimes, people realize that memory loss and lack of focus was the extreme attention to pain.
- The suntan acquired during therapy helps produce vitamin D and makes you look better.

To conclude the pain topic, when there is a health issue, people should stop and try to fully comprehend what the body is saying. Allow yourself the opportunity to get deep in the water, enjoy the body messages and your new course in life.

Chapter 14

Physicians as Facilitators

"If you are assisting someone else's birth, facilitate what is happening rather than what you think ought to be happening. If you must lead, lead so the mother is helped, yet still free and in charge."
Quote from the book
"The Tao of Leadership: Lao Tzu Te Ching Adapted for a New Age"
by John Heider

Physicians are NOT responsible for our bodies. Each one of us is.

Physicians are just universal resources of traditional science to help people in pain, using whatever resources they have, and with a promise to do it well, with the best of intentions. They can use a variety of resources, such as medications, procedures, therapies, and medical techniques.

But, what about our own responsibility for our own body and mental health? Physicians do what they know they can do. But giving the power of gods to physicians is irresponsible on our part as patients. Doing that is taking the power of healing away from the self. No one has given the doctor that godlike attribute but us. We have the power to heal with the help of science. It takes teamwork to get better. That is very real and true.

Some physicians are good, some are not, some are there for the mission, others are there for the title, to solidify their position, and for money. That is their choice, and it's ok. That's their reality, it's what they think it should be. But as patients, it's our responsibility to find the right doctor and the right assessment for assisting us in an illness, trauma, or pain.

Again, we must assume our own responsibility for our personal health as adults, and for the people around us. Let's be realistic. When did you start to leave your health up to destiny, without caring for it? How did you mess up your heart and liver with drinking, partying, doing drugs, overworking, or whatever else? When did you forget taking good care of yourself by sleeping well, exercising, taking time to relax and have some fun?

Physicians cannot fix with a pill the collateral damage you have done to yourself. Health collateral damage is hard to heal. A physician can assist you in making you feel better by taking out what is bothering you, or killing some nerves to help ease the pain. Sometimes, the shortcut of a surgical procedure does not really solve the problem. When shortcuts do not work anymore, the physical quality of life becomes impossible to handle.

Physicians can keep adding new pieces in your back, knees and shoulders, or wherever. But if you continue with your bad habits, that is your choice, not bad luck. And if you think nothing of it, when there's another complication, then you go back to get something else fixed.

The behavioral and mental patterns are there. Some people keep having things fixed with surgery, medication and, at some point, they may face a serious physical trauma or an emergency. Others change bad health patterns on time and the collateral damage is avoided. And other people, while trying to fix what's wrong with them, start feeling life is a pain, that life is awful, that physicians are bad, and these negative thoughts keep invading their mental health.

When you live life only surviving, and you never leave behind your negative behavioral and thought patterns, you are killing yourself. What about accountability for the self?

Why, if our body is the most precious vehicle the universe gave us to travel in this unique life, do we not take care of it? Why do we take the car, the boat, the motorcycle or jet sky for constant maintenance, paying for their care and parts, but we do not take care of our own, beautiful, only, and unique body model on Earth, until it crashes?

Life's health challenges due to trauma or accident are something different, medically speaking. With proper care, many people not only survive trauma, but also defy science and its methods. Why does that happen? I see it as a temporary break in life that gives people the beautiful opportunity to succeed and prove themselves in the realm of the universe. This can be done with the interdisciplinary methods of medicine and multidisciplinary methods within ourselves that can be learned and can be successful.

Louise Hay, one my favorite authors, who wrote *The Power is Within You*, puts this issue in a very special way when she talks about the body as a reflection of the mind. We respond physically to the thought of the conscious and the unconscious. How we think and see everything, we are likewise in the physical body.

Life's challenges always bring lots of blessings. Sometimes, we do not see them right away, leaving circumstances as they are without fighting them with love and conviction. Blessings come in different ways, and angels always come with them. I know hundreds of people that have gone through many health challenges, and all who have overcome the challenges have come to the same conclusion: you just need to open your heart, and the angels around you -including your physicians- will open the door to the right answer.

I lived an awful experience in the process of finding out what was affecting my health. At one point, I felt my life was at its peak. I was supposed to be in great health, but I wasn't.

That led me, in my ignorance, to feel rage against science and its representatives. But, had I not lived through that experience, I would have never panicked and paused to reassess my life. In that panic, I discovered myself. I understood what the real role of medicine was concerning myself, and my responsibility and accountability for my own life. The incident might be simple and irrelevant for some, but I exploded. Thank God!

Going back to seeing doctors as facilitators, let's remember that physicians are also human beings, who get sick and have ailments. However, it is generally known that even the best doctors, with brilliant careers, turn out to be the worst patients in terms of caring for themselves. Many doctors know this, acknowledge it, accept it, and even say it out loud. Plus, when doctors fall ill, they are unable to care for their patients, creating more stress and pain in their lives. This was especially true during the Covid-19 pandemic, where more than a few physicians retired early to avoid personal burnout.

Yet, there's a younger generation of physicians who have a more holistic approach to modern medicine, who do take care of themselves better than previous generations, and who are willing to recommend alternative therapies for their patients. I've had many cases of physicians coming to our center, and once they experiment the benefits of alternative aquatic therapy, they fall in love with it and want their patients to enjoy this kind of healing treatment for pain.

Take Dr. Juan (real doctor, not the real name), a high caliber neurosurgeon and director of Neurology at a teaching hospital. He was referred by an orthopedic surgeon after getting a calcaneus tibia repair. This surgery cost him days of inactivity, pain, loss of balance, inflammation, and lots of frustration because of constant interruptions in his professional and personal life.

He is young and otherwise healthy, so he knew little about self-trauma. He arrived to our center a bit apprehensive at first. But when he discovered how fast, effective, and painless his recovery was, he promised himself never to underestimate his patients' pain.

He was humbled by the alternative aquatic therapy he received, and he never ever minimized lack of movement. He now recommends to most of his patients getting this kind of dignified treatment. He is enjoying success in all aspects of his life and has become a better human being.

So, let's give physicians a brake and start assuming accountability for our bodies!

Chapter 15

Deep Water Monsters

Starting the Journey

When traveling through the most strenuous of times health wise, we encounter dark creatures and black holes that may do two things: they challenge the conscience and bring perfect light for the rest of the journey, or they kill your soul in the process.

What we are talking about here is how we can take advantage of available information, either against or in favor of our health.

When someone experiences deep confusing times, like an annoying pain, multiple symptoms, deep depression, or other health issues, the person does not fully understand what's happening, and then the black knights of the mind come charging in. These black knights start a quest against your best self-interest and confidence regarding your personal health. The worst are the ones that are waiting for you to start off in some state of pain, and then take advantage of your low energy levels and your vulnerability. They can carve the most scarring energy cyst within you.

I assure you that other predators will continue coming until you pause, go inside yourself, and talk to your body. The best lesson here is for you to gather yourself in time to prevent them from owning your peace of mind.

Predators of Knowledge

Close your eyes for a moment and you can see them chasing you. They tell you that you are not in control anymore because pain is the master.

To self-diagnose, you surf the Internet, you find a few pop-ups listing some of your symptoms and, just when you think you are downloading safe information, something hits you. You think you arrived at the right place, but instead you found the perfect predator of your will and your power to heal.

In this part of the journey, you need to decide on the wings you want to fly with. Do you want to escape and go to some other place? Do you want to stay for a while and study those predators? Do you want to see if that dark side is as dark as it looks? This is when your true self is going to act. Predators of information can be real traitors!

If you are scared at the beginning, you might analyze data and decide if, deep inside, you believe in it. You might get in touch with the apparent predator of information and ask if this is just part of the picture, or if it is the entire thing. Is this real, is it a creation or your imagination or, even worse, is it generated by your own knowledge?

You are now flying on your own. You own this experience, so you have the choice. There might be light if you stay for a while, look for clarity inside you, and ask your body how that all sounds. You can run and fly to another territory and explore other grounds of information. The information options are infinite. Still, the journey will prolong the same winds of uncertainty and the terror of thinking that you know too much. As Gyalwang Karmapa said, "value knowledge that is most useful right now… by how effective it is, not by how difficult it is to acquire."

When surfing the web, we are going to absorb mounds of information facilitated by researchers and physicians. It is information based on sample data and statistics, as well as scientifically researched documentation. The information might be written and published to be shared between physicians and researchers regarding similar cases and possible complications of illnesses.

Attempting to challenge those knights of science, without discerning the information, can kill your intellect and your possibilities of healing. That information is just a point of reference for certain cases amongst certain doctors, which helps them create some consensus regarding similar symptoms. But that does not mean that it is your personal reality or your drama. You can either accept the information or reject it. Pause for a moment and get a physician's assessment before you adopt any medical position that has nothing to do with your reality. We should respect those facts and examples, and find light in the physicians and their clinical thought behind them. They are the masters of light and science. That is finding light.

If you give some credit to your inner physician, you might encounter other possibilities. There are other plans: B, C, D, E. But keep in mind that needing to know more can ruin your reasonable doubt if what you read might not be for you. Also, if you decide to go the other way and start abusing your apparent knowledge, you may find other kinds of predators, and they are everywhere!

In my center, I have a rule that no person is allowed to recommend or offer any advice to another person in the facilities. I have encountered people that think they know a lot about every medical condition, and are always finding a victim to follow their advice. That is a very strong ego predator and an aggressive one. If they do not feel they're being heard, they can get nasty.

I had a case of a client suffering from herniated discs in the lumbar area. Let's call her Camelia, a forty-year-old. She came referred by a neurosurgeon with a note that read, "Please evaluate for water massage and aquatic therapy to treat severe muscle spasms affecting lumbar area." She is married to an oncologist and thinks she is one too. Her instructions at evaluation indicated that she had herniated discs at L4-5, S1. She said the neurosurgeon wanted to avoid surgery because of her age. She also informed me she had hidden spina bifida.

I had the results of her MRI in my hands, the ones that were reviewed by her physician. As I evaluated what she had told me, I saw a totally different reality than what appeared on paper. It was impressive to see how her own personal conviction of her condition drove her process. I recommended her to get craniosacral therapy.

The point here is that you should be very careful who you listen to and follow. Information is an ally at some point, the physician is your counselor in health, but you are the owner of your body. So, you have power over it.

Personally, I've been there, and done that! When I was diagnosed with lupus and fibromyalgia, I immersed myself so deeply in the subject that I almost drowned. I started to search the web, and read all the available books, all in less than a month. I was so amazed. It seemed as if all those books were written for me! Every symptom I had was documented.

I went as far as visiting the most recognized physicians, all with enormous egos and minimum compassion. One diagnosed me coldly and did not even touch me or talk to me. He simply took all my results and threw them on the floor. I was insulted and angry. I asked him who was going to pick them up? And his answer was, "the secretary." Oh, so macho! What an ass!

I relaxed and deleted all the wrong information from my body. It took a lot of me, with nutrition, emotional and psychological support, and exercise on land and in the water. Sounds so easy, doesn't it? Well, it was tough at the beginning, but I sure did get excellent results. Today, I have no trace of pain, no medication, perfect blood chemicals, and the most wonderful job!

Confronting the challenge of a health situation was disturbing, but it really was a blessing in disguise that resulted in what I am today. Through aquatic therapy, I have found healing, as well as my mission in life. I gained my freedom to be my best version, with integrated authenticity, and regained my persistent and most treasured mode of living my life with purpose.

Truth be told, it is all about fear, and sometimes we are afraid of self-empowerment. The predators are there to show us that we are the masters of our health. They show us the way.

The Pandemic Creatures

Pandemic creatures are like viruses. People have symptoms, but they hear some information by word of mouth and take it to be true and reliable. Your symptoms are well known by many, either because there is a genetic predisposition in the family, or because friends, who do not take care of themselves, have suffered some of them. The information, most of the times, comes from unsolicited sources, from pandemic creatures that can make you succumb in your journey by losing your strength.

The most likely place to encounter these dark creatures is in medical waiting rooms, where scientific knowledge is nil and opinions overabundant. It is an amusing circus to enter a physician's waiting room, where people love storytelling about sickness in the most frantic and horrendous ways. It is like a contest of who is suffering the most. I call this the fever of "big combos" (as in fast food). They want their illness combo to be bigger, so people feel more pity for them, and when they leave the physician's office, they feel they've won the "Victim of the Day" prize! Plus, they feel "good" because their condition is getting worse and they need more pain killers, especially after feeding the misinformation creatures. You can see that they even feel happier after the physician confirmed their health condition, and increasing their medication serves as a validation that they are the "winner". This is as toxic as any illegal drug!

Some people can be incredibly pandemic in their thought pattern, and in giving health advice. They can make up the most dramatic scenarios regarding health issues. They love having that "big combo" of suffering and drama. Deep inside, however, they are well intended. They can be very supportive and give their life for others, but sometimes their good nature excels as a self-destructive trait.

These are the strings of "good intention" that may kill you, unless you break the cycle. Cut those strings and keep floating in healthy waters.

The creatures in the doctor's office lobby keep growing and welcome new ones. They look like *Packman* characters. My daughter loves this comparison to the electronic game. It is a real dark space to be, but some people love it because they do not love themselves, and this is a way of feeling that they are being taken care of. This may sound funny, but it is very real and sad. Just watch it happen from a distance for a while. It would make me very happy if you do not like the journey from that perspective. You have a choice: pull away from these predators, or join the pandemic creatures and live unhappily ever after. Not a happy space.

Demons of Life

The demons of life are many and ugly. This predator is called the "diagnosis bacteria". Oh yes! When traveling around these demons, you are going to need an antidote to eradicate them from your life. This is the certainty of a scientific diagnosis and your adoption of it. When you get a precise and accurate diagnosis, it is impossible to avoid it.

A diagnosis can come with collateral damage if you do not follow proper advice. Some are accurate, some are not. But, what does your body tell you? Is it true? What is the collateral damage in your body? Here is where the angel of life starts to fight with the demon of life. You have the body, nobody feels what you feel. Medication and procedures will affect your body perhaps in a positive way, or maybe not. The doctor has an opinion, but you should use your inner physician to either accept the health contract or not.

I had a case of a nine-month-old baby boy, let's call him Marcus. He had Angel Syndrome with Infantile Spasm Syndrome. His doctors had diagnosed that he would never be able to walk, talk, move, nor anything else. He was non-verbal, screaming all the time, had poor neurological skills, and a very strong attachment to his parents.

Despite all his problems, his medical condition did not deter me whatsoever. I knew this baby had potential and could enjoy a remarkable improvement.

His parents were desperate. They lived on the other side of the island, but were willing to make the trip for the therapies, and were ready to refer other parents as well.

First, I needed the parents to see the same potential I saw in their son. Otherwise, they were going to sabotage their own process. Together, we analyzed each of the child's symptoms and, as we went down the list, they began to understand the role that their son's nervous system would play in the healing process.

We wasted no time to start working on this special case. In three months, the baby was showing marked improvement to the point that he stopped going to his regular physical therapy sessions. He got stronger, had more head control, his crying was easing, and he was eating better.

His parents started to truly appreciate the aquatic therapy process. It was exactly what they needed to experience so they could see beyond their current situation. Not only did we help them in the water, but taught them how to manage their son's condition and how to behave in front of him.

It was an amazing process for Marcus (not his real name, if you were wondering). He improved so much, that when his parents moved to Tampa, they wanted to find aquatic therapy services to continue his rehabilitation process. They found great support in everything, but alternative aquatic therapy for Spanish speakers was basically unavailable.

They came back to Puerto Rico and started the process once again. Six months later, Marcus was walking using a walker, talking like an adult, and going to pre-school.

As a family, they are now enjoying the miracle of life.

From that point on, I decided to coach parents that live far and have access to a pool to be their children's aquatic therapists. Once they gain the skills, they have them for the long run.

As we saw in this case, parents with physically challenged children know how to travel the way of light, regardless of the situation. Every morning brings a new light. They follow it, challenge all the predators, and continue the journey, never allowing dark creatures to succeed.

I must also say that there are many physicians with the courage to put themselves in the patient's position and say, "If it were my shoulder, I would not have surgery. If you do this or that, you can prevent the surgery." The patient has the option to choose the long road or the short cut.

Let's see this in a practical way. When you go with your car for maintenance and a check-up, you will ask and question what it will need, and you will ponder the cost, the benefit, the cost-effectiveness, and the risk. You should do the same when you go to the doctor. You have the right to ask and question everything when it comes to your body. Why not ponder the consequences and collateral damage in the long run? And why not find a second opinion? Why not ask for a plan B, without chemical or surgical procedures? Why not do some preventive planning beforehand?

Many people wade through these desperate waters, and the easiest route is to find a comfortable space where they can hide from the turmoil of negative thoughts. The choice is to reclaim the power of your health, and partner with your physician to find a good plan, and buy some time if it is not a dramatic trauma or illness.

Why not ask for positive outcomes even if it's not precisely the most common thing to ask. The winds may get dense and scary during a healing journey, but once they clear, the most incredible power of all emerges: you in command. Prepare your body for it, and do it now. Dedicating time and effort to your body is one measure that can ensure a better and faster recovery process.

There are people with all the odds against them that have succeeded in defying science, and not even physicians can explain why. The power of personal health is achieved by going to the light side and changing everything.

Many people have experienced post-trauma after a car accident, or have faced serious health challenges, just as I have. The common threat between them was that nothing seemed to stop the light in themselves. And even if they failed physically, they did evolve and grow.

Sometimes, all you need is just flowing stability, and that will take you further in your healing journey.

Chapter 16

Uncorking Life's Dreams

Questioning the truth, the dreams and the silence that screams for attention. Hearing the flood of thought waiting to be organized to direct energy in the right direction. Which is the right direction? What game are we playing?

The healing journey is self-explanatory. It is about thousands of hours of experiences in the water, with real results and lots of will to defy health circumstances. For some clients, with whom I have worked for a long time, healing with water therapy can feel a bit overwhelming. For other clients, life and time just seemed to stop in the water, allowing good healing energy to flow.

Time does not exist in the water because just one second may facilitate years of hard work, persistence, and patience. One second in the water may dissolve years of physical or emotional pain and trauma.

The clients we refer to in this book are real people, with different experiences and circumstances, and not necessarily wealthy. People invest their time and effort after being immobilized by desperation and pain. They have come in with physical and emotional trauma, chronic conditions, even nearing death. These are people with strong characters, willing to grow and surpass whatever life circumstances challenged them. The strongest cases are those of parents giving their hearts to defy the health condition of their babies or children.

I will also mention people lacking the courage to look inside themselves and start a new path, those who just followed the personal acts of self-terrorism and sentenced themselves to unhappiness. But I too must mention the people that have come and left, teaching me very profound lessons that changed my life forever.

These are my own masters of life, leaving with me the lessons of their experiences. Every day, when I get in touch with all the people I see, I heal myself and transcend to parts of life I never thought I would reach. These clients gave me the courage and the responsibility to write this book, and to share the information of how you can succeed, regardless of the situation.

These are people with abundance of love, courage and determination, even when their economic situation was not the best. A positive attitude in challenging circumstances has proven my point that personal scarcity has nothing to do with money. There have been very wealthy successful professionals who would give anything to have the emotional abundance of some others they meet in the pool.

People with little money can enjoy an abundant life and recover their physical health. Yet, others with all the money cannot get rid of the real cause of their condition because it goes beyond all that.

An interesting case of comparison is that of a wealthy man in his thirties enjoying the economic prosperity of a single young professional, living abroad, who was leading a hard-core night life. He suffered a physical trauma in a car accident, for which he had to be induced into a coma. When he came back to Puerto Rico, he had no choice but to go live with his parents, since he had become daily-task dependent. He was now being economically maintained by his wealthy family.

While he was receiving therapy, and started recovering, he would always talk about loneliness, sadness, and the need to live a new life. One of his expressions that impacted me the most was, "I want to live life in the light. I want to live in daylight, as I see other people doing. I've never had that. I have lived in darkness since I was a teenager, numbed by alcohol and drugs. My family insists I should socialize more with friends, but everyone I know lives in the dark side. I do not want to have dinner and see everybody drinking. I feel that would be going back to where I was."

He was obviously innocently sincere in his expressions, and he spoke with difficulty because of a slight speech impediment he had developed. The support from his family was not all there either. Even paying the therapy bill was an issue between his parents.

Sometimes, he talked to other trauma patients, and would very often meet with, let's call him "Carlos", another trauma patient who was not wealthy at all. Carlos' family struggled to make the arrangements to bring him to the pool. They would even change their work schedule to make sure that one of his brothers could be in therapy with him. He had two fine young brothers, with the biggest hearts I have seen. I cannot express my great admiration for them. Carlos' family offered their care with so much love, enjoying the process, and always staying close to him. Carlos' brother even became an assistant to us in the water.

This comparison between Carlos and the young, wealthy professional goes to show that no amount of money can buy love and attention.

Nancy's case (not her real name, of course) is another interesting one. She's in her fifties, healthy, working two jobs, and has four children with her only husband.

A few years ago, she came in to get therapy for pain in her neck and lower back. After a few sessions, she stopped coming and called me to tell me she was diagnosed with a tumor in her spine, at thorax level T6-T7. In addition to having to get surgery, she developed thyroid cancer.

She went through her medical procedures and came afterwards to get post-surgery passive therapy. She needed a lot of attention.

Soon after her surgery, she was held up in front of her house and the assailant threw her on the floor. She was hurt, but needed no intervention despite her recent surgery. Naturally, the incident traumatized her. She has always been high strung and stressed out, and this event did not help her state of mind.

She received therapy, recovered well, transitioned to active therapy, and she still comes to our center. About a year after she started exercising, however, she received the sad news that she had bone marrow cancer, which had metastasized, and was given no more than six months to live.

She was completely devastated. Being extremely religious, she asked me what I thought. Honestly, I was not prepared for this. The only words that came to me were, "Do you believe? You say all the time you do. This is the moment of truth. Nothing has changed in you but the name of the diagnosis." I told her there were many ways to improve her health with nutrition, meditation, supplements, etc. She followed through with all of them.

Eight years have passed since that terrible diagnosis. She is having the best time of her life, traveling, enjoying her grandchildren, loving her husband, and more importantly, loving herself more than anything. I admire her a lot.

My experiences with near-death clients, brought a new perspective to my concept about death. I have given death another name. I now call it a natural transcendence. Just as we have the right to be born in grace and peace, and the freedom to change and transform, we have the natural right to pass on to another existence in grace, peace, and ease.

Chapter 17

The Joy of the Effervescence of Life

Uncorking is a word I love because it explains how life can explode with beauty, passion and enjoyment. This simple word just opens my mind to a celebration of life, which is associated with champagne.

I used to work for the *Veuve de Cliquot* champagne brand in my marketing years. I had to study and appreciate the history, process, and finesse of the product, which goes beyond fine wine and liquor.

Champagne is an area in France that fascinates me, with centuries of history and mysticism. Champagne is also about sharing liquid celebration. It is a fine alcoholic beverage associated with romance and passion. I learned to love it. So, when I think of uncorking, I feel the sweet celebration of life's events. And in this chapter, uncorking is a celebration of health and renewal.

I feel the same celebration every time I get in contact with the ocean, especially in Caribbean waters. When I walk on the beach in the morning, I get in touch with the white effervescence of the water on shore. And when the waves come softly to caress my feet, it feels like the tingling sensation of bubbles celebrating being alive, of all my senses being stimulated, of the privilege of enjoying such a natural awakening in the realm of nature.

When I talk about uncorking in the water, I refer to letting go, to decompressing something trapped in the body. It is not only about attaining the best of the self with bubbly joy and happiness from each circumstance. It is also about freeing energy from tissue releases, from muscles, joints, fascia, even from feelings or emotions, as well as pain.

Yes, energy can uncork wildly and organically with water therapy, especially with Bio-Aquatic therapy. It is a natural way of uncorking and releasing deep conscious or unconscious matter in the body or mind. Without even talking, sometimes you can feel how a deep feeling, a lesion, or a cyst explodes for the betterment of the body and the person.

This is the same way water has opened the valve for me in the middle of my personal health crisis. I could have decided to accept my luck and do nothing, or do what I did to heal, create a new life and start the most wonderful life I could. I evolved in many ways, but mostly in loving myself. My creativity exploded with love for paint, writing, and aquatic therapy work.

In the water, during craniosacral therapy, despair and fear may uncork the sweetest compassion for the self. One of the most amazing cases I had was that of a fifty-six-year-old woman who showed up at my center, not knowing that the group she was going to join rescheduled their session for another day. So, I decided to offer her a free session. Providentially, I felt this was not going to be a fun class. The lady didn't look very happy and I did not know anything about her because she was essentially a "drop in".

On this first session, something really touched her senses. I was "Watsuing" her and she cried intensely. And at the end of the session, she could not stop crying. I could feel her body changing after several amazing releases during therapy. I felt some trust from her and a lot of letting go of something very profound, but she did not say a word. Her face changed dramatically, it was softer, but still seemed beaten.

Finally, she pulled herself together and told me what she was thinking about doing after her class. She had planned to commit suicide. Everything was ready when she got back home from the class. Nobody would be there, so no one could stop her.

I asked her how she was feeling after the session. She told me she had a personal conversation with God and she was given a new direction for living her life. She was desperate and depressed. After her husband died, she was left with a business, properties, employees, and an empty house. She had never worked before, and never dealt with any businesses or finances. It was all too much to handle. She continued coming to the exercise program, as recommended, for almost a year.

What was uncorked? Her self-worth, self-love, so much compassion was uncorked! She understood that she had all she needed to succeed. And she did! Right now, she is playing piano for a church, she sold the big house and bought a nice apartment, and she is traveling with her grandchildren, enjoying life, looking incredibly well and healthy. Passion for life and self-love is priceless.

Another experience of success, among many, is a client who spent six months in a coma after suffering post-sinus meningitis. When I first saw her, she was walking with great difficulty, pushing herself with just one leg. However, while getting her fourth craniosacral therapy in the pool, I was just at her hyoid bone when suddenly she started to move her legs like a race horse! I just allowed it to happen, and she did not say a word. I was so impressed. This lady had suffered high muscle tone almost to the point of incapacitation!

During the next session, it happened again. She said she could not control herself and asked me what was going on. I then asked her some questions about what she was feeling. She started to say that, while in coma, she felt she was falling and was scared, and she thought that running would prevent her from falling. It was a repetitive vision while she was in coma, like a dream she remembered.

That was simply compacted energy, uncorked with muscle relaxation. Later, she experienced better walking coordination, more stability, and was free of pain. She was so happy with the pleasure of movement and so amazed at herself. That was the start of her remarkable recovery. Her spirits lifted in an amazing way. She even tried to drive a few days later!

Uncorking also refers to releasing dreams, and even to our mission in life. Through therapy, mostly when I work with children, I have a profound conversation with the parents about life, the way their life has changed with their actual situation, about marriage matters, siblings and relatives. We also have conversations about how this situation might have a lesson for all, and what the options are to keep improving the life of these children.

I once treated a mom with a very complicated neurological condition. She was from the countryside. She was young, dedicated and, along with her very cooperative husband, worked very long hours to get her Certified Public Accountant degree. One day after therapy, we had a conversation where she told me she wanted to spend more time with her baby, and do something that could help him and others. She and her parents have a beautiful piece of land in the country with horses. There is no certified Equine Therapy center in Puerto Rico. Why not develop one? And there she went! Now she is in the process of doing something new and different.

There was another lady, forty-two years old, a Neuroscience Ph.D., former college dean, and manager of a neuroscience lab. She had a compromised neurodegenerative condition known as Spine Cerebral Ataxia, which was completely affecting all aspects of her life.

Through craniosacral therapy, she started getting better every day, and now is in the process of regaining her life, establishing a new business in Puerto Rico. This client decreased her medications and lowered her pain. She is now very well balanced and enjoying her family, her new life, with new projects, and lots of energy to share.

Is this an experience to celebrate, or what!

I can feel you are already wanting to jump in and get wet! Uncorking that bottled energy for the better is a pleasure for me. In the process of working with clients in the water, I transcend to my most intimate soul. My connection and flow uncork my creativity. My passion for water takes me to the most enlightened place in the universe. And it is bubbly!!

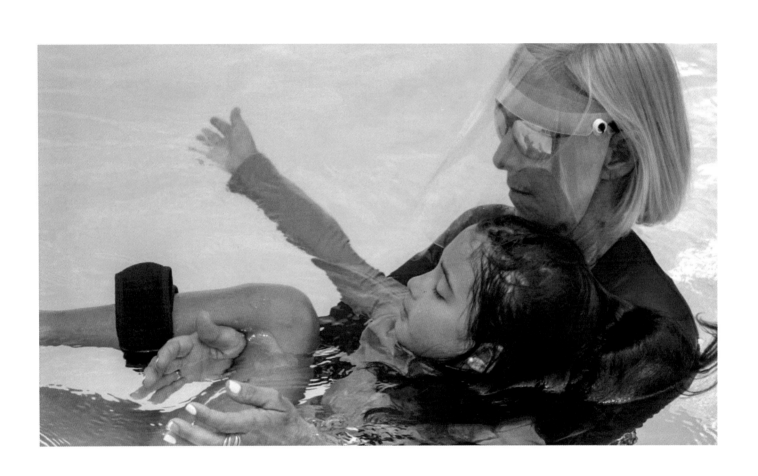

Chapter 18

The Memory Box Game

Immersed in a typhoon, circling without space or matter,
waiting for the moment of released light and life, only in water.

In everybody's life, there are always several boxes of memories we keep. A box might be beautiful when it holds a gift and we save it. A box may be kept for something we appreciate. We tend to attach feelings, sensations, or emotions to every event we experience in life. And we save them automatically in small compartments in the brain. When we do this, we hide those memories, store them in a dark place, and sometimes even forget where they are.

We tend to play and juggle with those mental memory boxes, much like the famous children's game *Memory*. At times, the memory compartments bunch together and create chaos, springing back like a Pandora's Box being opened. Other times, only one compartment opens and, boom! the explosion of that single little box brings more than chaos.

This is a simple way of looking at the unconscious. You can imagine it as a surprise memory box, bringing up vivid and disturbing concepts like fear, pain, nostalgia, uncertainty, frustration, and insecurities. Then you start asking questions to yourself, questions you used to ask before, but never found the answer.

Saved memory boxes are a very cumbersome equipment to fly with, much like traveling with heavy luggage. Holding on to them will never allow you to aim high enough to enjoy the ride or breathe clean air. In the water, a stored memory, even from childhood, may open and be released from the tissue for good. It might be a good or a bad memory, and it will work either way the moment the tissue is ready to release the right answer.

Ask yourself why you saved a certain memory. The answer will make you decide whether to throw it out for good, hide it again, ignore it as a part of you, or try to use it again. When you use it again, it's when you finally notice that, by saving it for so long, it has lost its function. You are ready to delete it, and you will understand why.

When you forget why you saved a memory, you understand that, instead, that space would have been available for other beautiful things. You should have burnt it from the beginning, disposed of it properly, as should be done with contamination.

However, there are situations in life -like a divorce or separation- that you think you've disposed all the feelings and memories about them. But the body of evidence still looms around and it's yours, and things you thought you have discarded come back at any moment.

The interesting part is that we tend to camouflage the extra luggage we carry about broken relationships. Emotional or psychological attachments are not about the person involved, but about all those emotions that the object of affection brings to your memory. When we remember experiences, we must keep in mind that they are just that, **ex**periences that we perpetuate in our lives, much like watching the same blockbuster movie again and again.

That is my message in this chapter. Start working on the memory boxes of your life and clean them out occasionally, just as we clean out a cluttered closet. We can envision these attachments as the entangled strings of a kite that create stagnant energy.

By the same token, complex emotions also generate new blockbuster movies of our lives, even changing the details of the story and creating new sensations that can damage your soul. As such, the experience must be put to an end, and the blockbuster movie destroyed.

The most interesting thing is that our own culture feeds this cycle perpetually, taking us to an *involution*, instead of to our evolution. That is the most dangerous thing in life. That is why we should be very good managers of our feelings, sensations, and emotions, because they trigger a very profound process in the brain that can even perpetuate from generation to generation. Cleaning out and looking closely at your memory boxes will expose who you really are, and will bring out the best in you.

Freeing yourself from these attachments and memories is a must in any healing process because they are strings holding you back from a happy journey. Water is a perfect space to find that freedom, to nurture your soul, mind, and body in a fluid way.

Somatic Emotional Release (SER) therapy in the water, particularly, has an amazing way to unleash this process of shaking off past attachments. Just imagine a dog gracefully shaking to dry itself and get rid of that excess water weighing down its fur, or a kite falling in the water, and then needing to dry off to elevate again and continue a flowing journey.

People must appreciate themselves regardless of cultural attachments, or social and emotional opinions. When we do this, our memory file gets slimmer, cleaner, more transparent, and easier to access without confusion. Emotional contamination can change and rot our spirit and personality. If it's not taken care of adequately, it can destroy us in *involution*. Ultimately, this is what happens if we do not expose emotions with an open heart; they will contaminate you and the ones around you.

As communities and societies, with so many unwritten tribal rules and ways of doing things, of having and being, we build up a general or communal emotional file, as well as an individual one. Sometimes, we engrave those rules in our souls without questioning, and the result is that we end up tethered to those rules, holding on to them, even when they hurt us.

From an emotional point of view, I am sure everybody can relate to this matter. But, what about all the hidden memory boxes that you have carried to survive for a period or phase of your journey? That has a price, and later in life, the body sends you the bill in the form of pain and discomfort. What I'm talking about here is how all the memories in the box relate to your body changing; how the body's ability to heal could easily change to an ability to self-destruct.

It has been proven that hidden trauma or experiences we do not confront will come back in some way. Sometimes it is accurate and smart to turn off on all those memories and just keep the good ones, the same way we refresh drawers and clean out storage closets. Also, staying positive, extracting the lesson and the happy stuff allows us to discharge the pain and rewrite the story. Events could be painful, but at the end, when we are open and conscious without adding emotional charge, we clear the brain and the body of unnecessary clutter.

I once treated a four-year-old child, who was forced-delivered at birth and his left arm did not have any movement at all. Even his posture, his crawling and walking were delayed by this condition. His right arm was hypertonic because he would overuse it. During craniosacral therapy, I noticed that the left arm was not dead. The child wanted to swim, and we needed to balance his body so he could do so.

Because he was forced into his current condition by a natural process, he accepted his reality and he assured me his left arm had no movement. While telling him "Ok", I stimulated both arms and felt a strong brachial resistance, yet he had some grip. In an interesting session, I held his right arm waiting to see some response from him and he suddenly tried to make some adjustments. I continued the process and he started trying to hold me with his left arm.

He loved the water and he learned to get his face in it and move around. I would always hold him from the left side. His left arm moved in a very subtle way, like a newborn baby in fetal position. After a few sessions, slowly but surely, he could move his left arm with some resistance and managed to swim like an ameba.

It was so much fun watching him. That process opened a space for him to look at himself differently and trust his body; to see himself improving and using his left arm more.

I firmly believe that he was awakened by the lack of resistance and the support of floatation, which assisted his movement in the water, much like in the womb. He was released from the concept of being born with a bad arm. He was perfect the way he was and became ever more confident.

Seba (let's call him that), now fifteen, still comes in for fitness sessions. He enjoys playing baseball and basketball, as well as participating in extracurricular activities.

This case that reminds me of my daughter's saying: "Imperfection is beauty and the idea of madness is genius." Who knows what happened in Seba's little memory box?

As adults, an excellent suggestion is doing a periodic hard disc clearance. It is so rewarding! Cleaning the emotional boxes is one of the greatest gifts in life. The Pandora's Box can be filled with bliss and happy thoughts. That is priceless!

Opening the Memory Box of the Body in the Water

The same way the **brain** is a memory box, which can play weird tricks on a person, the **body** can also be a perfect memory box. We can think the brain keeps the memory treasure, but no, it's not acting alone. The body has a whole hydraulic system running from the spinal cord, flowing through the heart, recycling the stream back to the brain and through the heart again at least five times a day. This is a scientific fact, so imagine everything that goes through the nervous system.

This presents another perspective on how the body does save memories in it. At one point in life, the body cannot hold any more memories, which can create restrictions and even illness.

The best way to describe this when I work with a body in the water is by imagining the spine and vertebras well aligned, like a stack of shoe boxes. They don't fall or push the others when in their normal position, but if you pull one shoe box out of the stack, the rest of the boxes move. A restriction in one vertebra is like that shoe box that was taken out of the stack; it will cause the spine to compensate and find it's balance to keep you moving. And this accommodation might result in pain in different muscles and even bad posture.

Without any intention from the person receiving therapy, while the therapist is working the tissue, everything falls into place. This technique of softly applying low pressure is used by chiropractors and osteopaths to leave an area released.

At times, this touch can bring back a memory that was stuck in that area. Suddenly the client tells you, "while you were in this area I remembered a fall, a situation, a person or something else." That is because the nervous system saves memories in different areas that can be released with therapy.

I remember one session where I was treating Samantha (not her real name either). She was feeling numbness, an electrical sensation in her left arm, and felt a sudden pain while I was giving her Bio-Aquatic therapy.

As I was working on her spine and moving her arm, she released the pain and the pressure was gone. At the end of the session, she told me that when she had the moment of pain, she remembered holding up her grandmother with that arm when she died to prevent her from falling to the floor, much like the case of another client I described before.

The best part was that she did not have to process any trauma. The body kept it and, through alternative aquatic passive therapy, she released that memory and the pain was gone. She got in the water and dealt with a trauma she thought never existed. She was amazed at how it worked.

This releasing of memories or past experiences may be disturbing to some and frightening to others, but if it is well managed, it is a glorious blessing to the entire body system.

There was another amazing case I had a couple a years ago. She was a thirty-two-year-old mother who had had two cesarean surgeries. She came to me after going to various physiatrists, orthopedic surgeons, and other specialists. This woman felt a lot of pain. It seemed to be a sciatic induced pain. Physicians believed she had hip problems caused by carrying and delivering big babies. Her abdomen was so swollen, she looked as if she had a baby inside.

During therapy, I was working her sacrum, and she remembered that when she was having her second baby, she was not asleep under anesthesia in the delivery room. She could hear the surgeons' conversation. She was in pain and told them so. They kept talking to each other and ignoring her. She felt a lot of pain during that process and, at the end, she felt she did not have the baby.

All those feelings came back to her during therapy. She told me she had expressed that to the doctor after the delivery, but he said nothing. She left the hospital with her newborn.

The baby was already three years old when she came to us. After a few sessions, she talked to her physician about feeling that something was inside her. She had a sonogram and everything was fine.

In her following sessions, she kept feeling a lot better. She started to lose weight, and she was not swollen any more. She had a lot of anger stored in her body because she felt the physicians did not treat her well during delivery. She felt ignored and abused by all the fun they were having while she was in so much pain. She felt the doctor's hand in her uterus. That was painful for her and she could do nothing about it. But she finally released all of it, and I'm so happy for her now!

In the water, memories unfold and open a door of wellness even without too much effort. The tissue can talk loudly and clearly from the deepest unfolded memories.

As can be gathered from the cases I mentioned before, I have observed amazing results in those floating moments, when memory unfolds to release a long-held pain.

It is so wonderful!

Chapter 19

Loving the Liquid Shadow - Perfection Within

I'm so happy at this time in life, the only person I need to impress is me!!!

Throughout our childhood and adolescence, we all played with our shadows. And some of us still do as adults! We would go to a place where we would have space and enough light to create our own shadow and play with it, moving and walking about, seeing ourselves from another perspective, from above and from within.

It is amazing to see your shadow's form and fluidity while it walks beside you. You feel regal and you never feel alone next to it. A shadow has a form that moves with perfect rhythm, with no specific pattern, color or style, changing in form and strength. It is like an aura of sheer marvel and greatness.

A lot has been written about the psychological concept of the shadow by many specialists. Here, however, it relates to the way it behaves in the water. In water, you are a silhouette that moves and reflects something. You are perfect. God made perfection out of you, and if you have any physical impairment, in the space and shape of a shadow, you do not have that impairment.

Debbie Ford's work about reclaiming personal power and transformation focuses on the psychological aspect of the shadow, but it is the polarity concept between the shadow and its creator that allows us to become a whole being. "And, as we let our own light shine," she said, "we unconsciously give other people permission to do the same. As we're liberated from our own fear, our presence automatically liberates others."

I was walking one day on the beach and young lady, fully clothed and with visible rheumatoid arthritis, passed by and shyly smiled at me. I returned the smile and, noticing her visible calcifications, her difficulty walking, and some pain in her face, I turned around immediately. When I looked back, I saw her shadow and there was no deformity. Then I asked myself, how does she see herself? In her shadow, she was perfect, fluid. The shadow did not limp.

Another day, I was walking on the beach again and shared my shadow's path. I was so graceful, happy, and light that day that I wanted to paint that sensation on a canvas. If people would look at their shadows instead of looking at social mirrors, they would be as happy as nature created them and as the universe wanted them to be, simply happy.

I tell my clients that talk about plastic surgery that, in their shadow, surgery would not make any difference whatsoever. The shadow would not notice it. The shadow knows nothing about flaws, wrinkles, color, scars, or pain. Life is easier in the presence of our personal shadow.

When you think of the shadow as your permanent companion, who needs company? Who needs a man, a woman, or even a dog (which is the closest thing to a friend giving unconditional love) when you have your shadow? You have your perfect essence right there, following you, unrestricted, quiet, supportive, amazing with greatness, reminding you of the perfection of the universe, believing blindly in dreams, passions, and your personal journey. The shadow never judges and is faithful, unless you deny it by trading it for a personal or social mirror.

The same happens in the water while I am working with someone. Both our shadows blend the same way the tissue does. We stop being two different silhouettes in the pool, becoming a whole mass of liquid shadows sharing the experience. The client is in prone position (floating face up), receiving, and my hands just meld in the head or any part of the body during craniosacral therapy.

During Watsu®, the figures disappear, the energy dissolves in the water and the blue shadow creates the most incredible fusion. Everything happens there, and then the shadows separate into individual forms, stronger than at the beginning. Watching the shadow can even be a supportive piece in the process of healing and nothing else.

In the healing process, this is a great trick for the mind to separate sickness or pain from the body. This helps the person detach from social parameters and accept the soul as it is, a magnificent creature of God.

So, love your shadow, embrace it, and then look at the mirror and say I love me dearly.

Chapter 20

Victory While Getting Wet

Success in the water is measured by intention, hard work and lots of love.

When I started looking for success cases for this book, I took into consideration a few common factors. The clue for considering success after a health condition is not going back to what the person was before. Success for me is transformation. A person starts a success process while rehabilitating, not from the point he or she was before the situation started physically, but from where this person started changing physically, emotionally, and psychologically. Success starts when the person understands this is a lesson to learn, that he or she needs to change something in his or her life. It even starts in the denial process, because denial will force the person to look for a different kind of help.

The catalyst will be the assumption of responsibility and doing their part in the game. The active and responsible act of willingness is what helps people succeed. The personal accountability to do what needs to be done makes a big difference.

Another factor of success is volunteering to risk the ego in the process of achieving personal growth and transformation. You must accept that the situation is what it is for a reason, even if you do not understand it now as such, nor its purpose. That takes away a lot of the ego pain, the "why me?" syndrome. Questioning things that will not provide an answer is an evolutionary process. There is not an accurate "Question and Answer" format for health issues.

The courage of acting and doing what your internal physician tells you what you need to do is just what it takes. Hear and understand the body's messages. Connect within the self and give the body what it needs. Stop listening to the negative voices of self-sabotage and self-pity within.

The successful clients I showcase here are people who enjoy and appreciate life more than before. They feel their situation was a gift and have done a great thing with it. Some are now healers for their own families. Some successful people have started a whole new career, a new path of life, a new job, or are now self-employed. These are big changes! Others have started a new way of looking at life, with a new perspective that has opened their minds and those of others around them. Some have simply been able to go back to their perfect physical body and to a whole new different life. They now share their lesson to help others around them or family members.

When choosing a case of victory, we are sharing a sense of confirmation of what is, should, and must be. Plainly and simply, when thought, desire, and will unite, they create reality.

Even though it sounds simple, it is not. Persistence and hard work will bring success in everything in life, even in matters of becoming a better person. Dedication, persistence, and resistance are winning factors in personal success. Yet, we tend to associate these aspects only in career and competitive fields. Clearly, I can say they are the most important aspects of success in life, including health.

If giving up is a looser attitude in anything in life, why give up on ourselves? Why not give the best and the maximum to the most precious person in the world: You!

Chapter 21

Stepping Up to Success

High reliability, High return, Not high finance.
Love is in the air, unconditional and selfish, forever, for me!!

What does the word "Olympic" bring to your mind? Games? World competitions? Ancient gods?

When I was working on this last chapter, I was vacationing in Greece for the first time. It had been almost two years that I had been working round the clock, with no time to rest, nor to relax and do nothing at all. Busy as a bee, I planned this trip of my dreams with my adolescent children.

I had always felt a very strong connection with Greek mythology. Venus, the goddess of love, laughter and beauty, was the name of my dog at the time. I thought I was letting go and forgetting about everything while vacationing in the Mediterranean, but life plays out in mysterious ways.

I bought a pair of books about mythology and history, but I could not get around to reading them. I was just immersed in so much live history, beauty, and fantasy. It was an amazing distraction. Yet, instead of fully enjoying this time off, I got busy working on this chapter, and it came to me as one of the most fluid ones I have written. It is amazing how the brain works!

I realized during that trip that life is an Olympic journey for all of us. My clients have their own challenges and I follow them as a coach, while dealing with my own trials. I see gods and goddesses in my clients, mainly because of their courageous attitudes.

When thinking about a rehabilitation program for a client, I often relate it now to the Olympic games. When you watch the Olympics, you feel the thrill of what is going to happen during competition. You are not there at the venue, but you admire the courage of these athletes competing and defying human records.

The same goes for a body lesion or ailment. You know there is no luck involved with treating these conditions; only persistence and dedication of heart and body can allow you to succeed in the category. During recovery, there are no short cuts. In a rehabilitation process, there is no intravenous injection, pill, or magic trick to make you move a missing part, a broken bone, or heal a trauma. Ask yourself, what does it take for Olympic athletes to participate in the game? The answer is determination, practice, dedication, certainty and trust in themselves, as well as investing in passion, and a lot of love for the game.

I see the same thing in my clients when they decide to follow their spirit and commit to their perfect health, just as an athlete accepts the challenge of competing. It takes all the courage of an athlete, and a lot more, because in the end, you appreciate and believe in the total and perfect plan of an Olympic healthy life.

I often talk to my children about the beauty I see in my clients, especially women. We women are so beautifully styled by God, with so much talent, grace and magnificence. I am so proud to be in this Olympic women's team of life! What's interesting about this feeling is that, originally, the Olympics were just for men. Women were not even allowed to enter a competition or train as athletes. What a waste! These men were just scared of women's natural magnificence and efficiency!

As with the Olympics, therapy is a one-shot opportunity to get over some condition, or maybe is just a significant opportunity to overcome a fear, or start life with a new vision. But mostly, it is the certainty of getting to know the perfect self behind a body and defying science in many cases.

When doing rehabilitation work in the water, I also understand how difficult it could be for those who do not even like the medium in the first place. Here, the choice is to follow all medical recommendations, and do everything in your heart to overcome the fear, panic, and terror of what is going to happen next. Just imagine how doing aquatic rehabilitation could feel when you panic about being in water! Here is the personal challenge I present to a person to change their perception in this case. Instead of hating water like a kitty cat, I convince them to let out their dolphin side and enjoy the game.

I always admire and respect a client's determination. That is what really challenges me and teaches me lessons every day. I put myself for a moment in that person's situation, trying to see over and above their physical condition, and measuring in a blink of an eye if they want to improve their health with all their heart. Then, I follow the process as a coach. I take advantage of their strengths, maximize them, and then I start working on the therapy. Ninety-five percent of the success achieved depends on the client's will and determination. Otherwise, I am just pushing against the infamous blue wall.

In the *Blue Wall* chapter, I explained how dreams can teach you about how life works and about your personal barriers. As an alternative aquatic therapist, I have learned, the hard way, that the process is not about what I can do, but what the client knows deep inside, and how strong a desire he or she has to make healing a reality. I am just a facilitator of that process, no more, no less.

As a client, I had my own championship tournament when my health was compromised. So, I know how it feels to be challenged that way. I felt the pain, the sadness, vulnerability, disability and "dis-ease"; again, not disease as in ill or unhealthy, but as in lacking ease.

Because I was an athlete in my younger years, when I faced my muscle-skeletal condition a few years ago, I remember thinking about not being able to move freely, about moving with pain, how sometimes parts of my body would cramp up. It was so frustrating! The worst cramp I had was the emotional one, the thought of someday being totally constricted. At times, I had to stop completely and wait until my body was rested, accommodated, and gave me permission to move. That was me as a "dis-eased" client. This is a concept I felt very deep in my heart. I understood it and applied to all aspects of my life.

Later, after my healing process, I began reading and learning more about it through other writers, such as Louise Hay and Carolyn Miss. Wow! I thought I had discovered something new. Now I live it every day with my clients. The more they heal, the more I heal.

During my dis-ease

I joined the swim masters league at the time, thinking that it would help my body. Believe me, it did not work. I thought I was not going to be competitive, that I would just participate for the exercise. Bull! Once I went to the first swimming meet, I put so much competitiveness into the race that I hurt myself and my hip cramped up. Right after the race, everything was fine. But when I walked to the car, my hip hurt so much, I had to control myself so I wouldn't cry.

The injury, however, was more serious than that. I had a lower back pain caused by the displacement of my hip. The loss of pride was even worse. The personal frustration about not being healthy then, and fighting against the situation, as I always did, was devastating. I thought I was no longer competitive at this stage of my life. I did not know how to give up. I had always been a fierce fighter, a worker, active, and going non-stop.

That was when I started to understand that my body has muscle memory. I started playing the way I did during my childhood and during my competitive swimming years. I would ask my competitive swimmer's intuition what I would do to sooth my cramps, so I could continue my journey. I remembered that when I was a child, I used to get strong cramps in my leg during swimming practice. I knew the coach was watching and he did not believe in excuses to stop practice, so I needed to reach the finish line, no matter what.

Immediately, an old wise body memory came to me. I received information telling me that I just needed to breathe deeply and get some oxygen to the part that was hurting. As soon as I did that, I started to feel relief. It is incredible what pure oxygen can do for your brain and body. Emotions were my handicap at this point, and it was not until I recognized the process that I started to heal.

It is funny how unconsciously Olympic the body can be. If we believe we have a perfect Olympic body, that body has its own way of healing.

Just being alive is an Olympic journey. Life is cyclic, passionate, and competitive. Constant mind and body training will allow you to surpass all types of obstacles to achieve success, prosperity, and evolution.

In my process as a patient, I remembered going inside my body, asking questions to my body parts, and giving them what they needed, because I understood that no one was responsible for my beautiful and healthy body, except myself. I knew deep inside what was wrong in my body, especially when I had been abusing it with lack of rest.

That may sound a bit weird, but it was so true. I had to watch out for my capacity to stay busy and to forget about restoring my body. I knew I had to take time off, float on my back, do my own therapy, stay for at least fifteen minutes doing nothing, not even meditating, just being. My body lovingly gave me gratitude with new energy and positive thinking.

Listening and paying attention to the body is sometimes the most difficult thing to learn day to day. The same goes for listening and paying attention to every thought we have. A lot goes on inside of us, but we do not pause to really listen.

In my experience and practice with chronic patients, I feel my clients have trained me to be a better human, to evolve and grow every day. I make myself practice everything I tell them to do. As a therapist, I lead by example, and every day there are more things I need to overcome, to learn, and achieve.

When I work with clients, I receive Olympic lessons of persistence, courage, abundance, and delivery that help me comprehend their individual situation. My commitment to the client starts with their reasonability and commitment to themselves. There is nothing I can do for them if they are not committed to their health. I am just a resource, a tool, a facilitator to help them achieve their healing goals.

I am totally convinced that the body is a perfect machine that knows everything.

Here are some of the comments I receive from my clients that decide to follow the process. These comments motivate me to coach them and cheer them on all the way.

1. *I know when I've arrived at the right place at the right time. If I do this, how would you assist me?*
2. *I only have this precious moment to heal, tell me what are we doing and when.*
3. *I have to stop medication and invasive procedures. I need to heal naturally.*
4. *I am here to begin healing. I am committed to whatever I need to do.*
5. *I know it will be hard at times, but I am committed to helping and doing whatever it takes. Where do I sign?*
6. *I am tired of trying, I want to heal.*
7. *I am not leaving without a therapy. Do you have the space for me today?*
8. *I cannot spend one more day feeling bad about myself.*

9. *When this happened I was indigent. But now I received some money from my grandma and I will use it to heal myself.*
10. *No doctor has touched me, but they are telling me I will never do (whatever) again.*
11. *I have this diagnosis but, I do not accept it and I am not crazy.*
12. *The past is gone, now is my time to solve this situation.*
13. *I need a push to start over.*
14. *I am seventy-two years old. I played tennis three times a week and did Zumba until the pain started. The doctor told me that my MRI shows spinal degeneration and that I should change my sport. I am seventy-two, that MRI is not me. I know I am old, but I am not stopping. Just get me back into the game and all is good.*
15. *The neurosurgeon told me that I had to stop playing golf and needed surgery right away. I will play golf and will do whatever to postpone the surgery. I cannot stop now.*

Sometimes, in an instant, I know if a client is going to make it or not. I would say that most clients who succeed in their Olympic rehabilitation process just have the guts to keep living, no matter what.

When treating cases of severe trauma or a life-threatening situation, what I enjoy the most is seeing the client's innocence come out, while letting go of their created persona. Sometimes even losing some neurons in the process of trauma brings back to life the innocence of our eternal child within. This allows whatever comes next to flow amazingly, with no further expectations, just the present day and vividly awaiting what is about to unfold.

There are five things that I always see in clients who will triumph in their recovery journey.

First, there is always a certainty, which I can read from the start. Even though they're in pain, they have the guts to say, "I will succeed". There is a confidence in a projected result, which is part of the process.

Second, there is a positive thinking pattern; frustration is not part of the game. Keep working and keep trying. We work like there is no tomorrow. We maximize the moment, letting rest and nutrition help in the process. What counts is having small expectations with great celebrations, hearing and feeling all the small steps.

The **third** and most impressive aspect of success is the gratitude involved in the minimum that is received; the sensation of being blessed by whatever is happening because there is a plan bigger than whatever we think. Gratitude is the most advanced and powerful attitude a human can have and, believe me, it makes all the difference.

The **fourth** element of success is the trust in yourself, in the grandiosity of nature, and your connection with it. Trust the amplitude of the body and its connection with what really matters in life. Understand how ephemeral life is and still maintain the desire to evolve no matter what, because there is a power over and beyond what allows us to create whatever we want.

The **fifth** and last element is hard work and dedication with personal commitment which nobody can do for us.

The researcher Masaru Emoto has conducted many laboratory tests regarding the subject of grateful and conscious healing in an aquatic environment. With his book *The Hidden Messages in Water*, he has made a great contribution to support scientifically the idea of the ability to heal through the spiritual consciousness of water. The beauty of love and gratitude reclaims our health and peace. Everything starts and ends with gratitude as the source of love. Masaru Emoto's studies discovered a world where science and spirit unite. He has proven that molecules of water are affected by thought, words, and feelings.

Remember that we are moving bodies made up of 70 percent water and our brains are 90 percent water. Can you imagine a more powerful statement?!? We have a lot of water in our bodies, but still we think we are so strong and solid, all muscles and bones. Not really.

The most important thing is that even thoughts go through the body's water, sending messages we are not even aware of. If we want to change that programming, we can do it. This is what can transform an intention to heal, into a *passion* to heal. Water vibrations and rhythms have a strong effect on our feelings and thoughts, calming or altering our moods. That is why using alternate methods of healing shocks everybody.

Let's appreciate the goodness of water. It heals us! Our entire system moves through liquid channels, through small tides that move in a soft way all the liquids in the body. Normal and easy functions of those movements bring balance, happiness, equanimity, and peace, facilitating our sense of stability, trust, harmony and resonance. That sounds so easy!

It is said that we are 99 percent water when born, 79 percent as adults, 59 percent when old. That is an interesting point of view. Getting old is a matter of water loss!! Just a joke!

Where there is no moving water, energy dies in the body or in life. Continuous flow purifies the water. Continuous movement generates more energy and life.

That is where inspiration comes from, from continuous flow inside and outside my body, with other bodies, with nature, with life!

I conclude our water healing journey with this quote from Donald Walsh:

"Change the way you want it to feel, rather than the way it feels, and what you think you have to accept. You are not going to stop change, you just stop change from happening the way you want it to happen. Just think about it, circumstances will keep arriving in life, everything else is up to you".

Let's Get Wet and Heal!

The Keys to Liquid Healing

1. Positive mental patterns are the power engine in this process.
2. Trusting the process and intuition facilitates every situation; we know what we need.
3. Recognize different factors, other than physical, that are not allowing healing.
4. Count your blessings during the crisis; the treasure of blessings is always immense.
5. Being 100 percent present in the body through the whole process of healing opens the infinite possibilities of organic healing.
6. Willing to quit medication bravely is just a matter of allowing the natural process.
7. Be patient with the progress means being compassionate with self-preservation.
8. Listening to the body and pleasing it with accurate actions demonstrates love, care and devotion to your beautiful creature.
9. Feeling grateful every day, and being open to whatever comes in the day, promotes happy surprises, filled with minimum expectations.
10. Sharing the experience positively with others with similar situations makes the load easier and lighter.
11. Have fun in the process of healing, laugh at the self and be able to rehabilitate.
12. Feel happy no matter what happens.
13. Be present and have no future expectations, but a positive present visualization.
14. Commit and be accountable by following through.
15. People are not the condition; the condition is only a lesson or learning process for a better being.
16. Laugh and love the self and be creative in the process.
17. Allow transformation of any type, you will be surprised of the gift behind it.
18. Share the story and cheer others on with love.
19. Do not try to understand. Just act, accept, heal!

In the end, it is all about falling in love with life and with the liquid, vulnerable self.

Suggested Reading

Amen, Daniel (2020). *The End of Mental Illness*. Tyndale House Publishers. Illinois.

Amen, Daniel (2021). *Change Your Brain, Change Your Life*. Tyndale House Publishers. Illinois.

Anodea, Judith (2003). *Chakra Balancing*. Sounds True. Boulder, Colorado.

Barral, Jean Pierre (2007). *Understanding the Messages of Your Body*. North Atlantic Books. California.

Chopra, Deepak (1994). *The Seven Spiritual Laws of Success*. Amber-Allen Publishing. California.

Covey, Stephen R. (2004). *The Seven Habits of Highly Effective People*. Simon & Shuster, NY. NY.

Hay, Louise (2007). *You Can Heal Your Life*. Hay House. Carlsbad, CA.

Heider, John (1985). *The Tao of Leadership: Lao Tzu Te Ching Adapted for a New Age*. Green Dragon Books. Lake Worth. Florida.

Love, Jennifer; Tore Hovik, Kjell (2021). *When Crisis Strikes: Five Steps to Heal Your Brain, Body and Life from Chronic Stress*. Citadel Press Books. N.Y., N.Y.

Nichols, Wallace J. (2014). *Blue Mind*. Little Brown and Company. Boston.

OSHO (2017). *Trust Living Spontaneously and Embracing Life*. St. Martin Press. N.Y., N.Y.

Robins, Mike (2009). *Be Yourself, Everybody Else Is Already Taken*. A. Wiley Imprint. San Francisco, CA.

Robins, Mike (2018). *Bring Your Whole Self to Work: How Vulnerability Unlocks Creativity, Connection and Performance*. Hay House. California.

Shojai, Pedram (2016). *The Urban Monk*. Penguin Random House. N.Y., N.Y.

Tolle, Eckhart (2001). *Practicing the Power of Now: Essential Teachings, Meditations and Exercises from the Power of Now*. New World Library. California

About the Author

Debbie M. Torrellas is the owner, founder, and creator of KinFloat® Aqua Wellness Center, the first and most successful alternative aquatic therapy facility in Puerto Rico. Because of her vision and pioneering spirit, she can be credited with establishing and developing the aquatic therapy industry on the island.

With more than twenty years of experience as a land and aquatic therapist, wellness and fitness Instructor, holistic health coach, motivational speaker and Brain Revolution coach, she has created her own therapy modalities, including AquaYogi® and AquaFlow®, which have made her center the most recognized enterprise of its kind in the Caribbean.

KinFloat® Aqua Wellness Center also holds an Aquatic Therapy University master degree certification, making it a formal university campus where aquatic therapy students can train and practice, and the only Spanish-speaking aquatic therapy campus in the United States.

Her dedication to supporting and motivating people to heal and pursue their wellbeing has transformed thousands who have found their inner physician through alternative aquatic therapy and now lead happier, more productive, and healthier lives.

Debbie is the mother of three successful creative entrepreneurs that also closely collaborate at KinFloat® Aqua Wellness Center.

She has authored three other books: The Water Kite Journey, *Vuela*, and Hole in One. Plus, she co-authored *Raíces* y Alas, a collaboration with a psychiatrist that highlights the cultural influence that grandmothers have in the development of the modern Latin woman.

Printed in the United States
by Baker & Taylor Publisher Services